THE
TALENT
ADVANTAGE

THE
TALENT
ADVANTAGE

HOW TO ATTRACT AND RETAIN
THE BEST AND THE BRIGHTEST

ALAN WEISS
NANCY MacKAY

WILEY

John Wiley & Sons, Inc.

ISBN: 978-0470-45056-7

Printed in the United States of America

10 9 8 7 6 5 4 3 2 1

To my mother and father, Jack and Roseanna Weiss.

—Alan Weiss

With love and appreciation to Rob, Garrett, and Devon, who bring me joy and happiness every day of my life.

—Nancy MacKay

Contents

CONTENTS

Contents

CONTENTS

Acknowledgments

I hereby shower praise and plaudits on the thousands of people in my mentoring and related communities who have kept me sharp, put up with my barbs, and joined me in the great learning challenge.

—AW

I want to thank all of my clients who have provided me with the opportunity to have such an amazing and fulfilling career. My thanks also go to Alan Weiss for his extraordinary mentorship and the transformational impact he has had on my life.

—NM

Introduction

What we hear from CEOs searching for top talent:

Employees are our biggest source of competitive advantage; finding and grooming talented people is our biggest challenge; we have all of the top talent in our industry; there are no other world-class people out there in our industry; we have to groom our own because we've had failures bringing external people into our company; recruiting companies aren't doing their jobs; we'll do our own informal search and we'll likely promote from within even if we don't have ready-now people internally; we don't have enough internal people to grow the business; the board wants us to hire externally because they think we are too inwardly focused.

What the research shows (McKinsey studies):

There is a world-wide shortage of talent and most companies are not prepared for the challenge of attracting, retaining, and developing people; talent management is typically led by HR and is not at the heart of business strategy; less than two-thirds of HR directors report to CEOs (due to lack of business knowledge), and they earn up to 50 percent less than peers in finance, marketing, IT; the influence of HR has declined significantly over the past 10 years.

Our work as executive coaches and consultants for the past 25 years shows:

Too many companies are not taking action at the CEO/senior executive level, and they delegate to HR; talent management is not a core competency of senior executives, and time and effort in this area is viewed as taking away from what they are rewarded for (growing the business); they are not held accountable for developing and retaining people; succession management and leadership development are not linked, and execution plans are rare; most senior executives were exposed to the sink-or-swim method of leadership development; new tailored approaches to internal/external coaching, peer coaching, job shadowing, mentoring, apprenticeships, and training are viewed as costs versus investments in people; silos get in the way of developing people; underperformers are not managed and are blockers for high potentials.

Role of the CEO:

The role of the CEO is changing due to the war for talent; winning the war for talent starts at the top with the CEO; CEO is the brand for attracting, recruiting, retaining world-class talent in your industry; CEO is the exemplar for striving for extraordinary leadership; CEO must play a lead role in building a leadership talent pool for competitive advantage; CEO is key to holding senior executives accountable for attracting, recruiting, developing, and retaining top talent; CEO must partner with HR to align talent management strategically; this book is about practical techniques and approaches to win the war for talent.

This is our attempt to bring a combined 50 years of consulting results to those executives who are in the talent wars and must gain that competitive advantage. Someone has to win. Heretofore, it's been our clients. Now, it can also be you.

—Nancy MacKay, PhD
Vancouver, British Columbia
—Alan Weiss, PhD
East Greenwich, RI
March, 2009

About the Authors

NANCY MACKAY

Dr. Nancy MacKay is president and co-founder of MacKay & Associates Advisors Inc., a consulting firm specializing in corporate strategy, organizational development, and leadership effectiveness. Nancy coaches and facilitates six CEO networks involving more than 70 CEOs. In addition, she operates forums for senior executives involving more than 50 high-potential executives. Her clients include Ritchie Bros. Auctioneers, Teekay Corporation, PricewaterhouseCoopers, RBC Royal Bank, Telus, Methanex, Best Buy, and many other leading organizations.

Much of Nancy's outstanding success can be attributed to her exceptional ability to collaborate with corporate management and help leaders get to the heart of what is holding their companies back. Her uncanny talent for identifying issues is matched only by her practical, straightforward implementation style.

Nancy has facilitated hundreds of workshops with CEOs, boards, senior managers, and executives. Her work as a consultant, executive coach, professor, and keynote speaker has taken her from New Zealand to Finland and throughout North America. She speaks at major conferences on organizational change, leadership development, and strategy.

A former university professor, Nancy has been on the faculty of the executive MBA program at Simon Fraser University and has taught at the University of Waterloo and Lincoln University in New Zealand. She has also been a visiting faculty member at the University of British Columbia.

Nancy is on the board of the Vancouver Chapter of the YWCA. She is a Circle of Care Member of the BC Children's Hospital Foundation and is a past member of Rotary International. She has also received numerous awards, including being named a World Class Consultant by an international group of her peers. Nancy was also named in 2008 to the list of "Canada's Top 100 Most Powerful Women."

Nancy holds a Bachelor of Mathematics and a Masters degree in Management Sciences, both from the University of Waterloo in Canada, as well as a PhD in Business from Canterbury University in New Zealand. She is the author of numerous scholarly articles that have been published in international research journals and many popular business publications.

ALAN WEISS

Alan Weiss is one of those rare people who can say he is a consultant, speaker, and author and mean it. His consulting firm, Summit Consulting Group, Inc., has attracted clients such as Merck, Hewlett-Packard, GE, Mercedes-Benz, State Street Corporation, Times-Mirror Group, The Federal Reserve, The New York Times Corporation, and more than 300 other leading organizations. He serves on the boards of directors of the Trinity Repertory Company, a Tony-Award-winning New England regional theater, Festival Ballet, and currently is the chairman of the Board of Trustees of the Newport International Film Festival.

His speaking typically includes 30 keynotes a year at major conferences, and he has been a visiting faculty member at Case Western Reserve University, Boston College, Tufts, St. John's, the University of Illinois, the Institute of Management Studies, and the University of Georgia Graduate School of Business. He has held an appointment as adjunct professor in the Graduate School of Business at the University of Rhode Island, where he taught courses on advanced management and consulting skills. He holds the record for selling out the highest priced workshop (on entrepreneurialism) in the 21-year history of New York City's Learning Annex. His PhD is in psychology, and he is a member of the American Psychological Society, the American Counseling Association, Division 13 of the American Psychological Association, and the Society for Personality and Social Psychology. He served as a member of the Board of Governors of Harvard University's Center for Mental Illness and the Media. He has keynoted for the American Psychological Association on two occasions.

He is a member of the Professional Speaking Hall of Fame® and the concurrent recipient of the National Speakers Association Council of Peers Award of Excellence, representing the top one-percent of professional speakers in the world.

His prolific publishing includes more than 500 articles and 30 books, including his best-seller, *Million Dollar Consulting* (McGraw-Hill). His most recent is *The Global Consultant* (with Omar Kahn; John Wiley and Sons). His books have been included in the curricula of Villanova, Temple University, and the Wharton School of the University of Pennsylvania, and have been translated into German, Italian, Arabic, Spanish, Russian, Korean, and Chinese.

He is interviewed and quoted frequently in the media. His career has taken him to 57 countries and 49 states. (He is afraid to go to North Dakota.) *Success Magazine* has cited him in an editorial devoted to his work as "a worldwide expert in executive education." The *New York Post* calls him "one of the most highly regarded independent consultants in America." He is the winner of the prestigious Axiem Award for Excellence in Audio Presentation. The *Providence Journal* wrote about him as "one of the top motivational speakers in the country."

ABOUT THE AUTHORS

In 2006 he was presented with the Lifetime Achievement Award of the American Press Institute, the first-ever for a non-journalist, and one of only seven awarded in the 60-year history of the association.

He has coached the former and present Miss Rhode Island/ Miss America candidates in interviewing skills. He once appeared on the popular American TV game show *Jeopardy*, where he lost badly in the first round to a dancing waiter from Iowa.

THE
TALENT
ADVANTAGE

CHAPTER 1

Why Leaders Must Fight the Battle

*Human Resources is to Talent Search as
Airplane Food is to Fine Dining*

The fundamental reason that leaders must lead the talent wars is that no one else is doing so within the organization. The acquisition of talent is not analogous to finance, or property management, or legal affairs, or public relations, which can justifiably be delegated to specialists.

Many organizations make the fatal error of entrusting talent acquisition and development to human resources, which is a fatal error. This function was once "personnel," or even "industrial relations," and dressing it up with the contention that people are "resources" that need managing from specialists is neither honest nor helpful.

Here's a quick test: Name five human resource executives promoted to CEO of Fortune 500 organizations in the last ten years. Assign that task to someone, and now let's get on with the rest of this chapter.

STRONG LEADERS ATTRACT STRONG PEOPLE

What do strong leaders do to attract top talent? Strong people are confident enough to surround themselves with strong people, and weak people surround themselves with weak people.

Years ago, we were brought in for the first time to Burlington Industries, at the time run by a CEO named Klopman. At the very first meeting, he revealed himself as a belligerent, nasty brute, ordering people around with obscenity-laced demands. At the end of the morning, as we resolved not to return, a colleague asked, "Why would his people take that kind of treatment on a daily basis?"

"Because he has surrounded himself with weak people who will accept that treatment, simple as that."

We believe that the readers of this book are healthy and confident and eager to build strong teams and cohorts. Here is some advice right from the outset:

1. *Build your personal brand in your industry—people want to work with people who are well-known in their field.*

3

Nancy MacKay worked as the executive coach with the newly appointed president of a division of a global transportation company to develop his 90-day action plan for his new role.

"I'm curious, why did you leave your big job at the competition to take on this new role with a much smaller company?" she asked. "And, you had to move away from your family and commute on weekends to see them as a result of taking this new job. Why did you do it?"

"To be honest with you, I come from a wealthy family so I don't need to work and it's not about the money. I've been watching this company grow exponentially over the past eight years since the new CEO was appointed. I've heard him speak at industry conferences, and I've bumped into him a few times at many industry events. When he approached me to join this company, I was ready to say yes because I know I'll learn a lot from him and one day I'll be the CEO of this company," said the president. Within six months, the newly appointed president was listed on the CEO succession plan, and Nancy worked with him on his development plan to be CEO "ready-now" within two years.

You want to serve as the magnet that attracts the metal and the mettle you need.

2. *Hire people who are smarter than you are. Your success is based on getting results through others, so why not put world-class people on your team.*

As input to a 360-degree executive coaching program, we interviewed all 12 board members of a large global manufacturing company to identify the strengths and opportunities for development of the CEO. This company was considered to be the world leader in the industry.

Talent Search

People are attracted to follow those setting an enviable example. They are repelled by those expecting people to do as they say, not as they do.

"The greatest strength of our CEO is that he is not afraid to put people on his executive team who are smarter and better than he is. He goes after world-class people, and he doesn't settle for anything less," said the chairman of the board. Every single board member identified this as the top strength of the CEO. And, every single direct report identified this as the top strength of the CEO. As a result, the entire company focused on attracting world-class people, which enabled the company to achieve extraordinary results.

Roy Vagelos, the now-retired CEO of Merck in its heyday, told us once after an executive council meeting, "I'm tough, maybe the smartest guy in the room. But what I look for are people who are smart enough and tough enough to challenge me. I always respect a good argument, and will change my mind as a result."

3. *Build long-term relationships with your stars. Always maintain relationships with your outstanding people whether they are in your own organization or not because you never know when they will come back to you.*

Nancy facilitated a three-day succession planning workshop with the eight-person executive team of a large financial institution. "Now that you've identified your top 12 list of potential successors and their development plans, how are you feeling about the strength of your leadership talent pool?" asked Nancy.

"To be honest, I'm not very impressed. If these people are going to be running this company in the future, I'm not sure I would want to invest in this company," said the COO. "There is no way we're going to meet our high growth strategy targets with this talent pool. I can't believe we haven't developed our people."

"We say our competitive advantage is our people, but clearly we're not walking the talk," said the VP of human resources.

Nancy challenged each member of the executive team to come up with a list of all the star performers they'd worked with over the past five years. Over the next six months, the executive team attracted five new external high potentials to the organization to strengthen their leadership talent pool.

In a consulting firm in Princeton, New Jersey, that was undergoing some bad years, Alan sat down with the senior managers with a list of 12 people. "They are all gone," noted a vice president. "How is this supposed to help us?"

"It's quite simple. If these dozen people had remained with the organization, we'd be three times our size today, because they are all doing spectacularly well themselves. The key is not to let this happen again, and to find the all-stars and make them productive and loyal."

4. *Success follows success—people want to work with successful people, and they will follow you forever.*

Nancy worked as the executive coach with the new CEO and executive team of a mid-sized, privately held retail company. The new CEO, who was previously the division president of a very large retail company, was brought in as a hired gun to take over from a family-run business. His mandate was to double in size over the next five years. Over the past five years, with the existing executive team, the company had experienced very little growth.

"You're going to have to build a new executive team if you want new results. Given your success track record with your previous company, you know where to go to get your new team," Nancy pointed out.

"They won't want to follow me here. It's a mid-size private company, and I won't be able to offer them the compensation that they want," said the CEO.

"They will follow you because they know you'll be a huge success in your new role and success follows success," said Nancy. Over the next six months, he replaced all but one member of the existing executive team with someone from his previous executive team. As a result, he exceeded his first-year business targets and was prepared for accelerated growth in year two.

It's not unusual for entire teams to follow their boss to new surroundings. There is nothing intrinsically wrong with this, so long as the team has a great track record and can adjust culturally. Blending imported talent and existing talent is a key leadership goal, and obviously not one that an HR department can be entrusted with.

5. *Get to know your competition. Build relationships and hire people who have "been there and done that" before at the competition.*

Alan works with many consulting firms around the world. When they need key resources, he asks whether there are people anywhere who have done what they need to have done. If the answer is yes, his advice is to go out and hire them, since we know that they can do it. If the answer is no, then the advice is to make sure that the expectations are reasonable to begin with.

Nancy worked as a strategy consultant with the president of a division of a large global company, who had seven direct reports. The previous year, the division was rated number one in the industry on all measures of success. "What's your secret to success?" asked Nancy.

"Over the past five years, I've recruited every single person on this team from one of our competitors to ensure that we beat the competition. We went from being rated top 20 to number one in our industry," said the president.

We've told our restaurant and hospitality clients: If you want to move from number 20 to number one, find the people who are working for the organizations ahead of you on the list. Don't try to reinvent the wheel. But you have to make sure you are attractive to them in more ways than mere compensation.

6. *Build long-term relationships with external recruiters. Short lists are getting shorter due to a worldwide shortage of leadership.*

If you build long-term relationships with external recruiters, you will get better service within shorter timeframes; make better cultural fits with candidates; make better decisions in selecting the best available top talent; and get top talent when you least expect it.

One of Nancy's CEO clients got a call from his external recruiter at a time when he was not looking to recruit anyone. "The top sales person in the industry has approached me to express an interest in working for you," said the recruiter.

"I'm not looking to hire anyone right now," said the CEO.

"He wants to make a move, and if you don't hire him I will have to send him to the competition. And, there might not be any top talent available when you're ready to hire someone," said the recruiter. After an extensive interview process, the CEO decided to hire the top sales person in the industry, which resulted in doubled sales in the first year.

Attracting top talent is a process that can't be confined to specific needs or organization chart vacancies. You want the best available athletes to come to you first.

THREATENED SUBORDINATES SINK THE SHIP

Weak subordinates are the first to run from trouble, to blame others, and to steal credit. They are invidious. The difficult, contingent action is to fire them, which is increasingly difficult and legally hazardous. The effective preventive action is never to hire them in the first place.

Here are the signs that you're losing this battle.

• *Create a fear-based culture. You cannot allow executives and leaders in key positions to maintain a "command and control" leadership style.* This sounds obvious but unless you create a sense of urgency for change, the shift to an empowering leadership style that attracts top talent will never occur.

Nancy was asked by the CEO of a large global company to work with his COO to help him build a more empowered leadership team and to attract top talent to the team. The CEO felt that the COO was very defensive and threatened by any comments from the CEO; a B-player with brilliant technical competency; a person with that command and control leadership style that created a fear-based culture that resulted in his inability to attract top talent to his team.

As a result, there were no potential successors for the COO. And, both the CEO and board felt the company was at risk given the declining operational results over the past year. Nancy suggested a six-month, 360-degree executive coaching program for the COO as a starting point. With significant pressure from the CEO, the COO reluctantly agreed to engage in the program. As input to the coaching program, Nancy interviewed the CEO, peers, and direct reports of the COO, which validated the CEO's perspective on the COO.

At the start of the first coaching session with the COO Nancy said, "Are you aware of your strengths and opportunities for development?"

"I'm the best person in the world for this job. I know I need to make a shift to empowering my team and let go of my command-and-control style now that we've grown to such a huge size. I know I don't have the right people on my team, but these people have been with me for a long time. I know I have to change, but I don't know how to do it and I'm going to need your help." Over the next six months, Nancy worked with the COO to attract both internal and external top talent to his team, to build an empowered team culture, and to develop strategies to improve operational results.

At a division of Hewlett-Packard, Alan was introduced to a notoriously tough executive in his last year of work prior to retirement. He was successful in terms of hitting his goals, but infamous for an authoritarian rule that left bodies along the road.

Once he retired, after making his plan one last time, there was no one within the entire division to replace him, because the strong people had intelligently transferred out long ago, the weak people stayed and followed orders exactly, and he had bothered to groom no one as a successor. He was a tactical success but a strategic disaster.

- *Hang onto under-performers—because they don't have the right mindset, skills, success behaviors, and experience to take on new challenges and attract top talent.*

Alan spent months with the president of a manufacturing operation in North Carolina convincing him that he had to fire his engineering vice president. The president felt that no one should fail "on his watch," which is a phrase that makes you wonder what the executive is watching—the psychobabble "good feeling" books or the business results.

After 90 days the resignation/termination was finally agreed upon, and both the president and vice president felt as if a weight had been lifted. The former went on to pursue his strategic goals, and the latter took a job with another firm where he was far more comfortable and appropriate.

If an executive is not firing poor performers, no one else is either.

Nancy was the leadership development and team effectiveness coach for the executive team of a newly appointed division president of a major financial institution who wanted his division to be ranked number one in the country. At the end of a two-day workshop, Nancy asked the president and each VP to commit to achieving the individual and overall team objectives that were set during the workshop. Everyone on the team made the commitment to deliver the results with the exception of the most senior VP. "I'm not sure I can commit to these targets given the uncertainty in my market, and my team is already working too many hours," said the VP of the largest region that was underperforming. "Let's take this off-line, given that we're out of time today," said the president.

Talent Search

All people are not equal and all opinions are not equally valid. The responsibility of leadership is to find the best and sort through the rest.

During the workshop debrief, Nancy said to the president, "It's clear that your senior VP is threatened by your goal of being ranked number one and he's not confident that he has the team to get him there. You'll have to work with him to see if he can shift his mindset and attract the right people to his team to deliver these results." Six months later, the president replaced the existing VP with a high-potential VP from another division, who was able to attract top talent to his team and speed up business results.

• *Ego-talk gets really loud.* That is, people who blow their own horns but don't choose to play in the company orchestra create discordant noise. We've found that these are the eight major ego-talk behaviors of threatened subordinates.

1. The Defender—I have a great team and they are all working as hard as they can.
2. The Genius—I know what I'm doing and I have all the answers.
3. The Blamer—I put everyone else, including the boss, down for getting in the way of success.
4. The Whiner—It's not my fault that my top performer got paid more by the competition.
5. The Cosmetic—I only reveal successes and hide failures.
6. The Controller—I'll take care of everything; trust me.
7. The Squirmer—Don't micro-manage me; I don't need a coach; we don't need meetings.
8. The Volcano—I blow up at people to cover their logical and factual ineptitude.

What you need to do about threatened subordinates:

1. Determine which subordinates are threatened by bringing in top talent.

    Nancy was the executive coach to the CEO of a large manufacturing company. He said, "I have a B-player sales

11

person who is going on a maternity leave, and she wants to move someone into her role that isn't a top performer. Her boss approved her plan, and I feel like I need to step in to make sure we bring in an A-player. I think she's feeling threatened by replacing herself with someone who might be even better than she is."

Nancy said, "Step in and help them bring in an A-player if you want to accelerate results."

2. Create a sense of urgency and hold subordinates accountable to participate in leadership development training and/or coaching and mentoring programs within a six-month time frame.

We worked with the CEO and executive team of a large global software development company on a team effectiveness program. During the first team session, the COO said to the CEO, "You need to stay out of our way if you want us to be successful. We've had a couple of bad quarters this year but that doesn't mean we need to bring in new people to rescue us. We know what we're doing."

The CEO met with us and the COO after the session and said to the COO, "You are a barrier to our success because you're threatened by bringing in the top talent that we need to turn this company around. I've asked Nancy to be your coach over the next six months as we make the changes necessary to bring in top talent. If you're not able to make the shift, then you won't be on the bus much longer."

3. Replace subordinates if they are not willing and able to make the shift within a six-month time frame.

One of Alan's CEO clients was having some challenges with his CFO. He said, "He's been with our company for a year now, and it's just not working out." Alan asked, "Is he aware of the issues you are having with him and have you been giving him lots of feedback along the way?"

He said, "Every time I give him feedback he gets very defensive and he blames me for not doing what he thinks I should be doing." Alan said, "You've waited six months too long for this decision."

STAFF FUNCTIONS ARE, WELL, STAFF FUNCTIONS

Staff functions aren't reliable sources for talent internally. Occasionally, the general counsel, chief actuary, or CFO gets the top job, but not often. And internal, lower-level positions are seldom filled by raiding the corporate staff areas.

One great exception we found was at Tastemaker, a global leader in food flavoring once owned by Mallinckrodt. The CEO placed the Mexican operation under his human resources vice president. "He has to learn," the CEO pointed out, "what his line clients are going through in leading P&L centers, and I'm obligated to try to prepare him for senior line functions."

But that kind of thinking is all too rare.

Staff functions such as IT and finance and legal attract people with a passion for technical competence, and all too often the relatively narrow education that accompanies it. (In the last decade, even MBA programs have significantly broadened their scope to embrace more diverse and non-technical subject matter.)

In most companies, the only way to get promoted is to move into leadership roles. That has created havoc, often creating the loss of a superb individual contributor and the concurrent creation of a lousy manager. IBM was one of the forerunners in resolving this carnage when they created the role of "fellow." In their system, a researcher could become a senior fellow, rather than be forced into managerial ranks. The ladder extended to executive fellow, so that compensation, prestige, and perquisites could accrue without undermining the talent bank.

But usually, technically competent people who would prefer to stay technically focused have no other options for promotion, and they take on leadership roles with no passion or competence to get more status, money, and advancement. The problem is that the company becomes a willing co-conspirator in this assault on competence.

Talent Search

If you blindly promote people from within, the cream does not rise until it sours. The milk goes bad long before that.

Staff functions lack accountability for P&L results so they are more likely to settle for less than top talent, and rightly so. When Alan worked with Merck for over a decade, the senior executives were fond of pointing out that they needed world-class bench chemists, but not world-class accountants. They were willing to pay for and pursue—with sometimes heroic efforts—the talent they needed in critical places, but they also recognized where "good" was, indeed, "good enough."

More recently, successful companies are putting strategies in place to promote, reward, and compensate people in specialized technical roles instead of putting them into leadership roles, as IBM pioneered. And in order to attract top talent in staff functions, companies are putting strategies in place to have people with strong leadership skills and a business background in charge of staff functions.

Examples:

- IT Functions:
  - There is a reason why CIO stands for "career is over" and the average tenure of a CIO is less than three years.
  - There is a lack of strong leadership skills in IT functions because most people are drawn to IT because they love working with technology, not people.

The CEO of a large global company fired his CIO after 2.5 years and replaced him with an internal business executive who had no IT background. When asked why he fired his CIO he said the following, "The CIO wasn't able to build relationships with the executive team, and he wasn't able to build and attract a strong leadership team underneath him. We made a big mistake by hiring for technical competence versus leadership strength when we hired him." That is increasingly the refrain today.

- Finance and Accounting Functions:
  - There is a lack of strong leadership skills in F&A functions because most people are drawn to F&A because they love numbers, not people.

    Nancy was hired by the CFO of a large global company to assist with the burnout situation that had been taking place in his department over the past year. The business grew very quickly, and the CFO was having great difficulty in recruiting top talent to keep up with the growth and increasing demand on his department. "What's getting in your way of attracting top talent?" asked Nancy. "We're an overhead department so I want to make sure we're only hiring for what we really need and we don't want to spend too much money on new hires because we have to set the example for the rest of the company," said the CFO. Nancy replied, "Top talent expects to be paid fairly, to have learning and growth opportunities, and great bosses who will provide an environment to help them achieve their full potential without burnout."

- Human Resource and Organization Development (OD) Functions:
  - This has become the dumping ground for people who are not good enough to serve elsewhere, and/or to prove the company's commitment to diversity.

There is a disproportionate number of minorities and women in HR senior positions. In fact, if you eliminated these people in the head count, you'd find the record of most companies in the diversity of senior people to be far more dismal than it is. Unfortunately, these people of tremendous talent have been relegated to the sidelines and are not in the succession plan beyond their silo. Moreover, there is a tendency to put people in HR and OD who are strictly theorists and faddists. They deal with training venders and create "team building" experiences that go nowhere and do nothing. As stated at the beginning of this chapter, virtually no senior executive in HR *ever* is promoted to COO or CEO, and the same holds true for lower-level promotions to line areas, which is why the Tastemaker example is so outstanding and rare. Transactional HR (benefits, recruiting, training) has been increasingly outsourced, and transformational HR (consulting, change management) has been increasingly ceded to external consultants with more expertise and less organizational baggage and political vulnerability.

- Strategic Planning Functions:
  - Unfortunately, what could be a very key contribution has become a refuge for theory and viewing from the sidelines.

    Why else would the strategy firms, from McKinsey to Alan's and Nancy's own companies, be called upon with such frequency to assist in organizational strategy? This area has become a *de rigueur* formality to please the board, but the only powerful executives who ever inhabit it are usually those a year or so away from retirement who need to be housed temporarily for benefits purposes. We have never seen a truly outstanding line executive be rewarded by an appointment to the strategy area.

Working with a $400 million animal health operation in Chicago, Alan was asked by the division president to work with the vice president of strategy (John) to improve his performance with colleagues. John sniped at everyone, blamed line management for the failure to meet his plans and, on close questioning, actually knew very little about strategic processes. He was an unsuccessful former line manager.

"Get rid of him," Alan told the CEO, after 30 days of fruitless coaching.

"Not on my watch," said the CEO.

"Do you really want to tell the board next month that you're 15 percent under plan and not yet able to open the European operation because you, personally, are spending 20 percent of your time on this guy's dysfunction?"

John was gone the next week. This staff area is usually the cause for more failure work than potential leadership.

WOULD YOU BE HIRED BY YOUR OWN HR DEPARTMENT TODAY?

We ask leaders all the time whether they honestly believe they (or people for whom they have a high regard) would be hired by their own HR departments today, as we return to our basic premise of why talent acquisition must be the key priority of leadership.

Here is what we've found, in summary.

The top ten reasons why you can't delegate winning the war for talent to your HR department and what to do about it:

1. *Lack of business acumen and financial literacy.*

   Key strategy: Companies are appointing people with line experience, on a rotational basis, to VP, HR roles to run

17

HR like a professional services business. This includes clear business objectives and metrics for success.

2. *Lack of understanding of strategic plan and business priorities.*

   Key strategy: HR has a seat at the strategy table to ensure HR strategic alignment with the overall company strategy. But this isn't just warming the boardroom chair. This means that HR performs the role of cross-functional synthesizer, looking at ways to marry career development and succession planning and proactively finding voids that must be filled by external talent acquisition.

3. *Lack of understanding of the skills, behaviors, and experience required for each role.*

   Key strategy: HR is moving away from an order taker role to a business partner role of understanding the business enough to be proactive in defining requirements for new roles. External help is fine, but HR must partner with superb external resources, not merely by books, software, and experiences.

4. *Lack of relationships with internal top talent.*

   Key strategy: HR is building relationships with high potentials and monitoring succession plan outcomes to ensure ready-now targets for high potentials are achieved. Once upon at time at the old Chase Bank, Rockefeller had a locked room with photos of "Chase Property," meaning the talent that had to be nurtured and retained at any cost. Supposedly, there were only three keys to the room. HR had better be living in that room.

5. *Lack of relationships with external top talent.*

   Key strategy: Hold HR accountable for building relationships with external top talent through involvement with industry associations and conferences. Some of the best HR people we've seen have a direct line to the top recruiters in the country. The sign of success: The company is presented with top candidates even though there is no immediate need, but is given the first right of refusal.

6. *Lack of accountability for business results.*

Key strategy: Hold HR accountable for outperforming industry success measures for HR benchmarks. In addition, HR becomes a partner with several line initiatives and they succeed or fail together. The traffic cop mentality has to end.

7. *Lack of decision-making authority.*

Key strategy: Give HR decision-making authority and accountability for delivering results similar to external recruiters. How many companies today are judging HR leaders by the tenure and performance of the talent they find outside or recommend from the inside after 6, 12, or 18 months in the new job? Not many? Are you?

8. *Lack of industry knowledge and key recruiting trends.*

Key strategy: provide industry-related training and development opportunities to HR professionals. They have to remove themselves from the HR silos in the profession and stop listening to academics or gurus with products to sell and speeches to peddle on how to implement the latest fad. Instead, they should be at the Harvard Advanced Management School, and conferences at INSEAD, and publishing their findings and intellectual property in business literature.

9. *Lack of sales and marketing expertise.*

Key strategy: Companies are creating VP roles accountable for both HR and sales and marketing to break down the silos and speed up recruiting. No one, but no one, should spend a career in HR.

10. *Key strategy.*

Consider dispersing HR into the line units. This is the most radical but we think the most promising and powerful approach. Stop thinking of HR as a staff unit, but think of it as a line responsibility for every line leader, no different from managing sales, or research initiatives, or product commercialization.

Talent Search

Get the troops in order. Either set HR on the right track or eliminate it, at least insofar as choosing talent is concerned. At best it's helping you, but too often it's hurting you.

In a major transportation company, we encountered the executive team pointing the finger at HR for not being able to recruit people fast enough to achieve the quarterly business results. The CEO agreed that we needed an executive team session to address the situation. "I'm holding every single executive team member accountable for recruiting top talent. The role of HR is to help each of you be successful in attracting the right people to your team so that you can deliver your business results. We're not leaving here today until we've come up with all of the possible strategies and execution plans to achieve our recruiting goals," he said.

If he had not held the executive team accountable for developing the recruiting strategies and tactics, the blame game would have continued with no new results.

Similarly, if you find that you wouldn't be hired by your own HR department, or top talent you already have found wouldn't, you have a problem. In any case, the ultimate responsibility is that of the leaders. You must work collaboratively with your subordinates, with external resources, and with HR (in one way or another) to ensure that you are winning the war for talent. Let's turn now to how you stack up.

CHAPTER 2

The Five Failings of Non-Extraordinary Leaders (and their cures)

The Leaders' Dysfunctions Become Everyone's Dysfunctions

Fortunately—and in our view, unbelievably—there is a handful of clear reasons why leaders fail to win the war for talent. In complex organizations, we originally believed that we would find matrix-like etiology that would make it impossible for us to easily advise our clients as to how to reverse bad trends.

That's not the case. There are five reasons.

PRIORITIES: NOT MAKING THE PRIORITY LIST

The lack of "ready-now" leaders has become a key concern at the board level in particular for high-growth companies.

We worked with a CEO and his executive team on developing a succession plan to accelerate execution of their strategic plan. The CEO kicked off the succession planning session by explaining, "We used to go to board meetings and the big concern was capital to expand the business. Now, we go to the board and they want to see who we have on our talent pool to expand the business. Our talent pool is our competitive advantage, and if we don't accelerate their development we won't be able to deliver on our strategic plan. Our succession plan is our number one priority."

In our experience (based on thousands of 360-degree executive coaching assignments), one of the most common development opportunities for CEOs, executives, and all leaders is *employees who want more coaching and mentoring from their bosses.*

What are the top five reasons why leaders don't make developing people a priority?

1. *Don't know how. I've never had anyone coach or mentor me so I don't know what to do.* There is an absence of role models, and too many leaders mistakenly believe they are running a boot camp for talent. "No one held my hand, I learned the hard way, and if you

fall along the path, you pick yourself up!" The problem is that even boot camps have drill instructors.

2. *Don't have time. I've got so much on my plate and I don't have time to "babysit people" on my team.* Everyone has the time. This is an issue of priorities and not resource scarcity. The time that's not applied is usually spent on such important things as meaningless and repetitive meetings, incessant number crunching, and failure work.

3. *Don't like doing it. My passion is building the business. I didn't sign up for coaching and mentoring people and I don't like doing it.* The answer here is to get used to it by developing the right skills and behaviors. Imagine stating that you don't like reading spreadsheets, or you don't like travel, or you don't like addressing the media. Too bad, part of the job, get good at it or find other work.

4. *Not my job. I thought HR was supposed to develop my people.* We've explained why HR is chronically poor in attracting and developing people, and why you, yourself, might not be hired by them today. This isn't delegation, it's abdication.

5. *Not on my scorecard. My bonus isn't based on developing my people.* First, that has to change immediately. But even in a more direct approach, how do you expect to meet the other items on your scorecard without the right people doing the right things at the right time? Put it on your scorecard.

What does top management need to do to make developing people a priority?

For high potentials:

- The CEO and executive team must develop a succession plan with clearly identified high potentials aligned with the company strategic plan. Think of the "Chase People" we referred to in Chapter 1. GE has been the embodiment of "bench strength" as terrific leaders have left the organization (e.g., Larry Bossidy to Allied Signal) only to be smoothly replaced by the depth of GE's talent.

- Break down silos by getting everyone to commit to developing the high-potential talent pool. For example, the CFO might be a mentor to the COO to develop his or her financial literacy.

Talent Search

The development of people must also be done *laterally* so as to create a culture of talent development that is not solely driven by vertical, silo-like needs.

- Identify the skills, behavior, and experience gaps for each high potential. For a long time, if you weren't going to manage an overseas operation for GE by your mid-40s, your career may well have plateaued. The company made sure that the requisite experiences were extended to its best performers.
- Create a development plan for each person on the succession plan to get them "ready now" by the agreed upon time frame (one to three years). See below for the most effective development approaches. Note that this has to be married to career development. In too many organizations the development of people (career development) is isolated from the strategic needs (succession planning), like two sides of a bridge roadway built from opposite shores that don't meet in the middle. Guess who usually runs career development? Human resources.
- For each high potential, assign an executive to be responsible and accountable for ensuring the success of the development plan. You cannot accomplish talent development without accountability. Who will be the mentor?

- Let each high potential know that, based on full executive support, he or she is on the succession plan; share future opportunities; and get input and insights into the development plan. In other words, allow people to take responsibility for their own development.
- Monitor results of the succession plan on a quarterly basis along with your strategic plan. Make sure the metrics are clear and are reflected in the evaluation of those doing the development for others.
- Cascade this approach down to all levels in the organization, right to the front line.

For all other employees:

- Provide development opportunities aligned with business strategies on an as-needed basis. This might sound harsh, but the development of the best people is the key to the talent wars. However, *ensure that the lack of development opportunities is not the reason for some people not being considered as top performers.*

Here are the development experiences our clients have had the most success with when used in a disciplined manner over time:

- *360-degree executive coaching:* Each executive and high potential works with an external coach to accelerate their development based on feedback from bosses, peers, and direct reports.
- *Coaching skills for executives and all leaders:* Executives and leaders learn coaching skills to move away from command and control leadership styles and to accelerate the development of the people around them.
- *Job shadowing:* Each high potential has an opportunity to observe and job-shadow roles that they are being developed for.

- *Internal and external programs:* Each high potential attends internal and external programs to fill skills gaps.
- *Individual mentoring programs:* Each high potential gets assigned an internal mentor based on skills, experience, and behavior gaps; they meet monthly by phone or in person for a one-hour mentoring session.
- *Group mentoring programs:* High potentials and executives participate in a group mentoring program to solve company problems together.
- *Peer coaching teams:* VPs meet once a month to share experiences.
- *High potential project teams:* Teams of high potentials are assigned projects to accelerate business results.
- Sabbaticals: Employees take a three-to-six-month sabbatical to study and/or have work experience to accelerate learning and growth.
- *External peer coaching forums:* Nancy is the executive coach and facilitator for nine CEO/executive forums involving over 100 CEOs/executives. YPO and other forums are excellent.
- *Peer best practices:* Alan has been able to bring global best practices to leaders so that talent development is an organic, continually improving dynamic.

ASSESSMENT: NOT KNOWING IT IF YOU TRIPPED OVER IT

Most performance management systems use the "bop on the head" annual approach. Once a year employees get "bopped on the head" during their dreaded performance evaluation and they learn about all the things that went wrong in the previous year and get told to fix it this year.

The converse is that employees save up, like chipmunks stuffing their cheeks, every perceived slight and mistreatment over the past year, ready to unload them at that single evaluation meeting. It is irresistible force and immovable object.

27

As you can imagine, this approach results in significant retention issues!

Nancy began a coaching assignment with the CFO of a company who had just had his first dreadful performance review with his new CEO. A year earlier, the CFO had applied for the CEO role and didn't get it because the board decided to bring in an experienced external CEO.

Nancy asked, "What was so dreadful about your performance review?"

The CFO said, "He told me I would never be a CEO because my people skills aren't good enough, and he gave me a list of all the things he considered to be my weaknesses. I think I need to quit my job even though I've been with the company for 10 years and I love this business."

Nancy replied, "Is this consistent with your 360 feedback?" He said, "No, my direct reports love me, and I get along really well with my peers and the board."

The moral, of course, is not to allow one person's opinion to get in the way of your ability to make a contribution to the organization. Instead, develop an action plan based on the feedback and go back and ask the evaluator to meet monthly to check in with your progress.

In this case, three months later the CEO got fired and the CFO was promoted to CEO.

What are the most critical success factors for performance management systems?

- Create trust and candor with your direct reports. Ask the question "On a scale of 1(low)-10 (high), where are we on the trust and candor scale? What can I do to move us to a 10?" And provide examples: 1 = "Even if you praise me, I ask, 'What does she really want?'" 10 = "You might request something unreasonable, but I'd still do it without question because I believe you have my best interests in mind."

- Clearly define and share the outcomes that you are responsible and accountable for with all of your direct reports. Make your role transparent, so that you can be held accountable, too.

- Ask each direct report to define outcomes that he or she is prepared to be responsible and accountable for. Focus on clearly defining agreed-upon outcomes. This is a dynamic process that changes throughout the year as new priorities get assigned. Always be on the same page regarding outcomes and priorities. Compare notes as conditions and priorities change in the business.

- Clarify expectations and overall company targets. For example, a simple framework:

  A—exceeds expectations (20 percent)

  B—meets expectations (70 percent)

  C—does not meet expectations (10 percent)

Note that there are only three possibilities. If almost all of your employees are exceeding expectations, which many weak evaluations systems would claim, then the organization had better be having an historic year!

- A player will want to know very specifically what it will take to get an A, so take the time to clarify expectations. Make it qualitative, not just quantitative (e.g., *how* clients are handled, not just *more* clients handled).

- Hold a team meeting to break down silos and share all outcomes and interdependencies for everyone on the team. Get people to commit to individual and team accountabilities. Allow the team to self-sanction its progress, holding its own members accountable.

- Hold quarterly performance management meetings with all direct reports. Ask each direct report to self-assess his/her performance based on agreed-upon outcomes. Review the assessment together and build on strengths. Identify opportunities for development if there are gaps in performance. Ask for feedback on what you can do to be a better leader.

Talent Search

No evaluation session should ever come as a surprise, because feedback should occur informally on a weekly basis and formally on a quarterly basis. It's that simple.

- Provide ongoing coaching, mentoring, feedback, praise, and recognition throughout the year so there are no surprises during performance management sessions. Note that this should be accurate, not balanced. That is, negative and positive are not relevant; accurate is relevant.

- If your direct report is not meeting expectations, work with your direct report to determine if it is a skills, behavior, or experience gap. Either put a plan in place to address the gaps or find a new role for this person. Hoping for new results over time without an action plan is one of the biggest mistakes leaders make. And unlike the Hawthorn Experiment (which was dubious to begin with), people do not necessarily improve performance just because they think you are paying attention.[1]

EXEMPLAR: SETTING THE WRONG EXAMPLE (COGNITIVE DISSONANCE)

The leader has to serve as an example to others in securing talent. How is it done?

Nancy was coaching a newly appointed CIO, and he had just received the employee engagement scores for his department. His IT department scores were more than 20 percent lower than the overall company scores. Nancy said, "The good

---

[1]These experiments were meant to show that employees worked better when the lights were raised at a plant in Hawthorn, New Jersey. But it was found that they also worked better when the lights were *lowered*, which the researchers claimed demonstrated they worked better just from the attention they were receiving. In fact, the experiments were seriously flawed, but they are the darling of human resource departments.

news is you've inherited a team that you'll really be able to work with to raise the bar on the engagement scores. The lowest score is related to retaining the key people you need to achieve your objectives. Why do think that is?"

He said, "I have no idea, but that's HR's problem so I don't want to spend any time worrying about that issue."

Nancy responded, "That is exactly your problem. It's not up to HR to attract, develop, and retain your people. You and every single person on your team are responsible for doing so."

The CIO finally admitted, "You're absolutely right. I'm really well-connected to people in our industry and in our profession, but I don't think any of my team members have any external relationships. They probably don't have too many internal relationships either, given that we're losing key talent. I guess we've got a lot of work to do in this area."

What are you doing to attract, develop, and retain top talent?

CONNECTIONS: CAREER DEVELOPMENT DIVORCES SUCCESSION PLANNING

One of the most common mistakes leaders make is they don't stay in touch with high potentials and they give them up to HR for development. This is a mistake because high potentials need a lot of new challenges and learning and growth opportunities to stay motivated—otherwise they get bored and feel they have to leave the organization to get new challenges.

The leader's role is to stay connected and assist your high potentials in achieving their full potential. HR's role is to provide the most effective tools and approaches to accelerating development once you've determined the career plan for your high potentials.

Nancy was coaching one of her CEO clients and she asked him to describe his approach to developing his executive team. He said, "I have four A players, three B players, and two

C players. I don't spend any time with my A players because I don't want to get in their way. I spend some time with my B players to try to get their performance up. And I spend most of my time with my C players because I have to tell them what to do in order to get them to deliver results."

Nancy pointed out, "According to your 360 feedback results, you need to spend time coaching and mentoring your A players and you need to move the C players off your team if you want to retain your top talent."

Alan has consistently found, in working with more than half the Fortune 500 firms over 30 years, that the preponderance of development time, money, and energy goes to the C players. It is remedial help, trying to bring myriad employees up to "average."

To win the talent wars, leaders must do something heretofore counterintuitive: They must invest the great preponderance of their attention, time, and resources on the A players, who can drive the organization forward and thereby create a tropism that draws the rest of the organization toward those standards.

Talent Search

Walk into human resource, organizations development, or any other staff area that has developmental responsibilities, and determine if they are basically investing in excellence or mediocrity. You'll be surprised and unhappy at what you find.

Key strategies for staying connected with key hires, and ensuring they are challenged at the high end:

- Let your high potentials know they are on the succession plan and the potential future opportunities that were identified for them by the entire executive team. Put some pressure on them to live up to expectations.

- Work with each key hire to help them develop a 10-year career vision that freaks them out (or at least jazzes them up). Most people achieve less than 10 percent of their full potential, so really challenge each key hire to play a bigger game. Ask them this: If you knew you couldn't fail, what would you be doing 10 years from now? Force the "stretch," and eschew conservative plans. The idea is to be on the radar screen, not avoid it.

- Identify the skills, behaviors, and experience gaps for the career plan. This need never goes away, but is often simply not done.

- Partner with HR to validate the career plan and to identify the most effective development approaches. HR has to help or get out of the way. It would be best if they helped.

- Provide full support in terms of time, money, and resources for your high potential to follow through on the development plan. The excuse that someone is too busy is an immediate red flag to reorient the mental set of those involved. The leader must exert this pressure.

- Hold high potentials accountable for following through on their career development plans. This must be a joint effort, not something merely done to them.

- Provide coaching and mentoring on a weekly basis in addition to quarterly performance reviews. We've said "weekly" before. We mean it. This must be a normal aspect of your communication and conversation.

WOMEN: NOT UNDERSTANDING MALE FILTERS

According to a study of 353 Fortune 500 companies conducted in 2004 by Catalyst, companies with a higher representation of women in senior management positions financially outperform companies with proportionally fewer women at the top!

33

Dr. Helen Fisher's research on more women at the top indicates that they will speed up the transformation of companies from command and control to collaborative and empowering cultures due to the difference in male/female styles of leadership. (Alan has appeared with Dr. Fisher on the agenda of the American Press Institute. In comparing notes, they found that women are often better equipped for leading and developing others because they tend to have less ego at stake and are more empathic. However, their drawback is often that they take conflict too personally and don't sufficiently allow their views to be heard in unpopular or unfavorable environments.)[2]

Interesting news: More women are being graduated from universities than men. Bad news: There are declining numbers of women in senior management positions over the past 10 years (e.g. Canada has gone from 26 percent to 22 percent of senior women at the top over the past 10 years, according to a Statistics Canada study).

In the United States, the trend is not understood because of the "glass ceiling" rhetoric, perpetuated by political leaders. Alan has identified the phenomenon of "glass walls," wherein women are promoted in designated areas, such as HR, finance, PR, and law, but are unable to move laterally to operations, manufacturing, sales, or other line areas. It is rare to find women as the senior executive in those line areas, even today.

Both men and women need to be aware of the male filters and behaviors that exist and get in the way of women getting to the top and thriving at the top.

The chairman of the board of a large global company said to Nancy in confidence:

"We have 150 people on our leadership talent pool—only five are women and none of them is on the executive team. We have a serious problem in this company, and I'd like you

---

[2]See Dr. Fisher's book, *The First Sex*.

to work with our CEO to develop a strategy to increase the number of women on our leadership talent pool."

Nancy asked whether he had talked to the CEO about his concerns. He had, many times but with huge resistance. The CEO always says his all-male executive team would never buy into spending time on dealing with this "minor issue," given all of the other priorities they have and the male-dominated nature of the industry.

> **Talent Search**
>
> Women are essential to winning the talent war, but they must be able to break through glass walls and be accepted into all aspects of the organization.

Building awareness of male filters is the first step in moving things forward. Nancy was doing a two-day leadership development program with the CEO and his executive team. She made a suggestion that they include the topic of creating a more female-inclusive work environment on the program and see what happens. Nancy reported back to the chairman and he was delighted to hear that the CEO agreed to include this topic on the program.

On day two of the leadership development program, Nancy presented the Catalyst 2004 statistics and the following 10 strategies, which are based on hundreds of interviews with women over the past 10 years, for companies to create a more female-inclusive work environment.

1. *Watch your language.* Swearing, inappropriate humor, and sexual comments are not part of the solution. Whenever this is done in the presence of a superior officer, it is tacitly approved by his passivity. Such behavior must be stopped at the moment it occurs, not later, not secretly, and not delicately.

2. *Pick your spots.* Get feedback from both men and women about social activities and venues to hold business meetings. Simply ask yourself if you are seeing females in key meetings. Hewlett-Packard has been one of the most gender-blind organizations we've worked with, and it was never unusual for Alan to be meeting with 20 people, 18 of whom happened to be female. No one thought twice about it.

3. *Foster a more collaborative work environment.* Men and women have different and equally valuable communication styles. Women thrive in a collaborative versus command and control work environment. They also have to be assured (and develop the skills to understand) that disagreements are professional, not personal, and situational, not permanent.

4. *Hire women.* For male-dominated industries, be proactive in setting quotas for having women on top-three lists for recruiting. At Merck we called this "heroic action." You can't rely on traditional HR avenues and approaches.

5. *Promote women.* Women don't get promoted like men do. Women in leadership positions are exemplars for others. Women often have to prove themselves a lot more in comparison with male counterparts, in particular for P&L roles and succession plans. Be proactive in setting quotas and providing external coaching for women. For example, in Norway, all publicly held companies must have 40 percent women on their boards. Many companies have a recruiting policy that states there must be at least one woman on every short list for senior positions. In order to accelerate leadership development for women, many companies provide external coaching for executives, high potentials, and all women in leadership roles.

6. *Pay women.* Ensure women are paid fairly relative to male counterparts. There is no excuse for unequal pay for equal jobs and merit. None.

7. *Establish a formal mentoring program for both men and women.* Note that this should not be gender-specific. We've found that strategies calling for women to have solely female role models and mentors are specious. The key is *excellence* in role models and mentors. (Alan has mentored Nancy for five years at this writing.)

8. *Promote life balance.* Implement policies to promote better balance between work and life for both men and women.[3]

9. *Ensure parental leave policies are competitive.* And ensure they are available for men as well as women.

10. *Create a more flexible work environment.* Most women don't have stay-at-home husbands, so they need more flexible work arrangements when families are involved.

11. *Establish a women's affinity group.* These groups typically report to the CEO and are led by the most senior female executive. They involve conferences and/or special events to promote relationship building and networking opportunities for women and exposure to both male and female senior executives.

After the two-day program, the EVP of HR challenged the executive team to develop an action plan to address all of the issues presented. The VP of legal was in full support and said, "Guys, to be honest, I haven't had the courage to challenge all of us to step up in this area because we've been doing things that I think could get us into trouble. But now that it's out in the open I know we have to change the way we do things, and it's time for all of us to take this seriously."

The CEO took accountability to work with the executive team to develop the action plan and present it to the board at the next meeting.

---

[3]See Alan's book, *Life Balance: Converting Professional Success into Personal Happiness* (John Wiley & Sons, 2003).

What are the critical success factors for creating female-inclusive work environments?

- Board and executive team understanding of the *business case*.
- Leadership commitment to setting the priority and building awareness of effective strategies.
- CEO and executive team awareness of effective strategies.
- Leadership commitment to the development of a strategy and execution plan.
- Involvement of men and women in the development of the strategy and execution plan.
- Resources allocated and monitoring of outcomes related to the execution plan.

This is how to overcome the dysfunctions. Now let's examine the key priorities.

CHAPTER 3

The Three Priorities of the Talent-Seeking Leader

How to Accelerate and Simplify the Search for Top People

We provide you here with proven approaches to strategy development and execution with an emphasis on attracting, developing, and retaining world-class talent as the key to competitive advantage and the acceleration of business results.

That is a mouthful. But we're not trying to make a case for simplistic approaches or easy thinking. "Reengineering" has a ring to it, we admit, as does a book title such as *Execution*. But even the late Michael Hammer, the creator of the reengineering movement (or at least its popularizer) had to return a couple of years later and amend his work. By his own admission, he had underestimated the people dimension and was responding to criticism about it. Charon and Bossidy talk about almost nothing other than people in their book, *Execution*.

Some years ago, we were asked to work with a large New York financial institution to assist in a change management project. Since I have always refused to help with "downsizing" work (which is always a poor contingent action to atone for executive strategic errors or inattention), I asked to sit in on an early meeting to assess the environment and dynamics.

Throughout the early part of the meeting, a human resources manager kept talking about "attrits," which we thought was some kind of financial product they were reducing or eliminating. It wasn't until she mentioned "minimizing severance options" that we realized she was talking about people. "Attrits" was a bizarre cognate for attrition, and the group was subconsciously attempting to avoid dealing with the real issue: throwing people out in the streets.

After the meeting, the senior vice president dismissed the group and asked us if we thought we could help.

"The first thing would be to get rid of HR's role in this and stop talking about 'attrits,'" we told him.

"We can't do that," he explained. "This is our primary strategy."

"Then I'm not your guy—good luck!" Alan said as we ran out of the office and the building. They did undergo a massive layoff, but did not recover their profitability until a massive executive purge years later.

On another occasion, we were at a major insurance conference and were invited to visit break-out groups during the afternoon. In one such session, a COO was explaining "parking employees."

"What does that mean?" Alan asked, wondering if a COO was really concerned about where people put their cars.

"Rather than saying we're downsizing," he said, "we talk about 'parking' people until work can be found, either internally or, more likely, externally. Of course, after a certain amount of time elapses, their severance will run out if there is no external opportunity. What would you call it?"

"Deception," Alan said. (And this is why he is always paid in advance.)

Talent Search

There is no such animal as a company with unhappy employees and happy customers. And there are no happy employees if their talents are not being developed and exercised on the job. If they get their kicks playing saxophone in a jazz band on weekends, that's not helping your organization.

Let's get to the priorities.

WINNING THE WAR FOR TALENT: PEOPLE

World-class people attract, develop, and retain world-class talent. Most people probably achieve somewhat less than 60 percent of their full potential, left to their own devices. World-class people strive to achieve 100 percent of their full potential, and can come close to it if nurtured and supported by attentive leadership.

Those who we're calling world-class people develop winning strategies and create a culture of accountability for results.

The key issue is that they can do this themselves, in a self-directed manner, which decreases management's need to constantly monitor performance. So who are these rare birds?

What are the attributes of world-class talent?

1. *Passion for the business*: Have a strong personal connection to the business. Over the past three years, we have been working with the CEO and executive team of Ritchie Bros. Auctioneers on leadership development. Every single person on the executive team (and their direct reports) has a total passion for the business, which is what enables the company to be the world leader in their industry.

2. *World-class mindset:* Always strive to be a world leader. Over a one-year period, we worked with the CEO and all leaders at Teekay Corporation on leadership development. The CEO and every single person on his executive team had a world-class mindset, and as a result Teekay Corporation is recognized as an international leader in energy shipping.

3. *World-class team:* Build a team of world-class talent. GE has been a leader in "bench strength" of the highest degree. The United States airlines, with the exception of Continental and Southwest, have demonstrated the opposite: thin bench, a great deal of movement from company to company, and underperformance over the long haul.[1]

4. *World-class competence:* Commitment to life-long learning and achieving their full potential. Organizations with this talent and approach to talent offer sabbaticals, community work, and pro bono "lending" of executives to add to their learning and meet personal growth desires.

---

[1]This has nothing to do with the price of oil. Herb Kelleher at Southwest and Gordon Bethune at Continental stood head and shoulders over an industry of midget leaders who could only make money if times were perfect, which times never are.

5. *World-class employee engagement:* Commitment to world-class results versus industry average. Gordon Bethune brought Continental Airlines from last to first in business preference travel by offering bonuses to *every* employee if three indices were met: number one or two in the industry in on-time performance, baggage delivery, and customer satisfaction. GE under Jack Welch had a stated strategy of being number one or two—no worse—in any business it owned, or to sell that subsidiary. (One wonders how NBC has continued to be one of their properties at a time when they are selling their historical appliance division.)

6. *External contribution:* Commitment to making a contribution to their industry, community, and profession. Organizations such as Levi Strauss, FedEx, and Hewlett-Packard have actively engaged in community and social work that allows employees to make contributions to the social and physical environment within the auspices of the organization.

7. *External recognition:* Recognized by external peers as world class. Life is competitive, as is business. Money is not a motivator (though its absence is a demotivator). If you give an unhappy employee more money, you have a *wealthier* unhappy employee. Accolade, award, and acknowledgment are important for world-class performers. Just watch the victory lap after a runner wins a world championship.

Talent Search
You don't put thoroughbreds in the back of an old barn or feed them table scraps. You establish a regimen, an environment, and attentiveness that ensures they are able to reach their full potential.

Most investment and attention in the world of organizations is lavished on the mediocre and average, in an attempt to improve performance remedially. That's the exact wrong approach. Outstanding leaders first recognize what world-class talent is and then create the environment to develop and attract it.

STRATEGY DEVELOPMENT: INVOLVING THE RIGHT PEOPLE

The quality of your strategy depends on your ability to involve the right people in the development of your strategy.

Prepare yourself for success in strategy execution (which is where failure occurs most of the time) by ensuring effective involvement of all key stakeholders. Strategy development done properly is an effective retention and development initiative.

A Brief Digression

Strategy always is successful in formulation, because it is a conceptual exercise done in a comfortable room, usually in a lovely resort, "facilitated" by a skilled consultant who can take ideas and create orderly easel sheets. The result is a lovely three-ring binder, usually in several colors, which proceeds to gather dust on the dozen or so shelves of the participants in the meeting.

Strategy fails in implementation, because that is where the difficult transitions occur to translate strategy into operating realities. At such critical juncture points, accountability is usually missing. We can count on the fingers of just two of our hands the organizations we've seen that hold top leaders responsible for specific implementation steps for strategy, in terms of performance reviews and bonuses.

1. *The role of the board*

> The board signs off on strategy. The CEO and executive team are accountable for developing the strategy,

since they will have to implement it, but the board has the governance responsibility to both assess the wisdom of the strategy and evaluate executive performance in achieving it. Common challenge: The board wants to have influence on the development of the strategy; executive team wants autonomy to develop the strategy.

Recommendation: Involve the board in the development of the strategy to ensure full support and sign-off. This needn't be in formal meetings, but can often take place in one-on-one interviews or informal discussions. One of the primary subjects must be the type of talent the organization will require in the future, and how it is to be attracted and retained.

2. *The role of the CEO and leadership team*

The top players must understand the external environment (Porter's model is a fine one: competition, suppliers, buyers, threat of substitutes, and new entrants) and three-year key industry trends. (Going beyond three years, and in many cases even two, in these times, is an exercise in dreaming and guesswork.)

The team must obtain agreement on internal strengths and weaknesses and external opportunities and strengths, of course, at a minimum. Secure agreement on your competitive advantage from a customer perspective: customer service; innovation; cost-effectiveness. Achieve agreement on your competitive advantage from a people perspective: leadership talent pool and strategic job functions. Obtain agreement on three-year success measures, and develop tactics to achieve them.

Talent Search

We've been in too many organizations where the board and executive team act like competing soccer teams, except there is no referee, so some fouls take place without penalty. These two groups must be on the *same* team, and that takes place only through collaboration.

46

3. *The role of the chief strategy officer*

Where this job exists, it should lead the development of the strategy. That includes the building of relationships with key industry players, thoroughly understanding the developing external environment, and working with division presidents and subsidiary heads to develop strategies. (Note that this position is often used as a dumping ground for executives whom no one wants elsewhere, and that winning the war for talent demands a very talented person in this job, not someone who is unable to do anything else.)

4. *The role of high potentials and succession candidates*

Invite these people to participate in the strategy development sessions. Include them as a part of the process instead of merely a subject of the process. Assemble a team of high potentials/succession candidates and ask them to develop a draft strategy for consideration within the overall strategic process. Make them part of the dynamic for their own growth and success.

5. *The role of employees*

Every employee ought to understand the strategy in order to provide input and, most critically, to execute the strategy. Years ago, we were working with the Associated Press to help improve performance. It was not a strategy project, but one involving the improvement of the organization's talent and productivity. I asked, at one point, if there were a current strategy document guiding behavior.

"Of course," pointed out the senior executive present. "It's right here within reach," and he pulled out an admirably brief, glassine folder from his drawer and handed it to us.

After we looked through what appeared to be an intelligent approach, well configured, we asked what the employees had contributed and what they thought of the resultant plan.

47

"My God," said the executive, "this is confidential. We'd never show it to the employees!"

You can't make this stuff up.

STRATEGY EXECUTION: CREATING A CULTURE OF ACCOUNTABILITY FOR RESULTS

In our experience, 90 percent of all strategies fail because they never get executed.

Nancy worked as a strategy consultant with the president of the largest division of a global transportation company, who had ten direct reports. She worked with the team to develop a three-year strategy and a one-year strategy execution plan. Three months later, the president's biggest concern was that the team was not delivering on the results of the strategy execution plan.

"Do you meet with your team on a monthly basis to review the status of each objective on your execution plan and to hold them accountable for delivering results?" Nancy asked.

"Well, we said we would meet monthly to review the execution plan, but we have had other priorities come up and we haven't been sticking to the monthly schedule," said the president. "I just don't understand why people don't deliver what they say they are going to deliver."

"Have you delivered on all of your commitments?"

"I guess if I haven't been holding monthly meetings and I haven't delivered on my commitments due to other priorities, why would my people be any different?" admitted the president.

Creating a culture of accountability for results starts at the top. I also worked with that president and her team on a monthly basis for the next three months to create a culture of accountability for delivering the results on the execution plan.

Here's why teams fail on strategy execution:

1. *Not enough trust and candor on the team*

Ego gets in the way: People over-promise and under-deliver because they don't want to admit that they don't have the skills, time, money, and/or resources available to deliver the results. They fear the admission that they agreed to a plan that they really had no idea about how to execute (or, worse, any interest in executing).

There is too often a "bop on the head" culture: People get bopped on the head when things go wrong versus a "what can we learn" culture, so we don't repeat the mistakes of the past. In too many organizations, people get whacked for making mistakes. Alan worked with a huge hospital that had signs on all the walls stating that one of the key values of the organization was "respect for people." (These are all preprinted in some "successories" operation, somewhere.) You could see managers figuratively whacking people right in front of the signs. The CEO announced that he couldn't understand why the organization's valuing of people hadn't translated into better trust and candor.

"Bill," Alan asked, "do you think people believe what they read on the walls or what they see in the halls?" No one believes what they read or hear in organization life, they only believe what they *see*.

> **Talent Search**
>
> Don't make the mistake of not trusting people because they are not good performers and thereby trusting no people. World-class people, by definition, are people whom you can trust. If you can't, there is something wrong with them or *you*.

2. *Too many priorities*

A lack of reality testing: People get attached to their favorite strategies versus what's the best way to achieve the desired outcomes based on the limited time, money, and resources available. You might call this the bandwagon approach, and it seems to have infested the American auto industry since sometime in the 1970s, as it steadily lost first its global lead, then its domestic lead in car sales. Customers and clients validate the worth of any new product or service, so here's a conceptual breakthrough: Why not try asking them *first* before inflicting someone's brilliant idea on them?

We love to talk about Akio Morita "creating" the Walkman, but that has proved the exception. All too common is the Pontiac Aztec SUV, the design and existence of which are almost totally unfathomable.

3. *Silos*

Being stuck in silo mindset: Every member of the team needs to step into the shoes of the president during strategy execution to get everyone set up for success to deliver team results. Leadership has a dual role, one of which is *corporate leadership*, and serving as the exemplar thereof.

We once worked with State Street Bank in Boston, which, at the time, was in four clear silos. The head of the investment silo, the largest contributor to profit, acted as if he were running his own company and openly defied his colleagues and even the COO as the spirit moved him. This seriously undermined the organization's ability to move strategic initiatives forward.

For years, Hewlett-Packard's printer division head (that unit and printer ink, believe it or not, was by far the most profitable part of the high-tech organization) held a de facto veto over corporate initiatives since no one wanted to mess with either his unit or his head. The threat to the bottom line was just too immense.

4. *Lack of accountability plans*

Most people understand the boss's accountability expectations—you hold yourself accountable to your boss for delivering results. In order to achieve team results, people need to understand:

- Individual accountability—you hold yourself accountable for honoring your commitments.
- Team accountability—you hold yourself accountable to your peers and they hold you accountable for joint commitments.

Most organizations seeking to do team building don't succeed (other than having a nice day rappelling down small hills or building sand castles at the beach under the tutelage of highly paid consultants) because *they actually have committees*. That's okay, committees are often more appropriate, but you can't "team build" a committee. If you desire true team accountability, then no one in that team can succeed or fail more than any other member. That is, rewards (and punishments) are joint. If some can succeed more than others, then you have a committee. Get used to it.[2]

5. *Lack of commitment to achieve results*

Commitment is "I'll do whatever it takes" versus "I'll do my best." This is no small issue. Focus on commitment to success versus all the things that could go wrong and excuses for not delivering results.

If a phone rings at 5:05, there are three things that can transpire.

1. Someone who has done their best is already on the elevator on the way out, having done their best for exactly eight hours, not counting lunch.
2. With advance knowledge that the phone will ring at 5:05, the boss can demand someone stay, cajole someone to stay, or pay someone to stay to answer it.
3. Someone who hears the phone who is not rushing away from their desk rushes back to answer it.

All of this seems quaint in a day of answering machines and e-mail, but the metaphor holds: A real commitment to achieve results often means going beyond one's best and doing what actually needs to be done. That can mean

---

[2]In brief, teams share resources, ideas, credit, and so on. Committees share only to the extent that there is no real sacrifice on the part of the donor.

performing unpleasant jobs, or stretching beyond one's presumed capabilities.

Here are our suggestions for the CEO role in creating a culture of accountability for results:

1. Work with your executive team to develop a one-year strategy execution plan aligned with your three-year strategic plan.

2. Ensure that the execution plan has five main categories of objectives: financial, customer, operations, people, and IT, with clear accountabilities for each objective (see Figure 3.1, the execution plan template).

3. Ensure that each individual develops a one-page accountability plan aligned with the execution plan (see Figure 3.2, a sample CEO accountability plan); this is a living document that gets revised throughout the year as accountabilities change. (Get rid of job descriptions, which are typically out-of-date lists of activities with no accountability for results, strictly inputs with no outputs. You might as well list "put on the coffee pot" or "shut out the lights when you leave.")

A final example: Unlike most companies, Best Buy created a culture of accountability for results using a bottom-up approach. The goal of the initiative called ROWE (results-only work environment) was to judge performance on results instead of hours.

The idea started with a handful of employees who wanted to boost morale and productivity in order to beat the competition. The vision for ROWE was that performance would be based on output instead of putting in time at the office. Productivity went up an average of 35 percent in departments

Objectives	Lead Responsibility	Involved	Strategies by When
Financial Objectives			
#1	ML	AB, JS	Strategy 1 by Q1
#2	ML		Strategy 2 by Q1
#3	RG		Strategy 3 by Q3
Customer Objectives			
#1	GB		Strategy 4 by Q1
#2	GB		Strategy 5 by Q2
#3	GB		Strategy 6 by Q3
Operations Objectives			
#1	GB		Strategy 7 by Q1
#2	RG		Strategy 8 by Q2
#3	ML		Strategy 9 by Q4
People Objectives			
#1	JH		Strategy 10 by Q1
#2	JH		Strategy 11 by Q3
#3	GB		Strategy 12 by Q4

Figure 3:1 Execution Plan Template

CEO Value Proposition:

Restore ABC company to strong financial health, and position the company as a leading company for long-term growth and shareholder value.

Goals:

1. Ensure execution plan objectives are achieved.
2. Develop and support a strategic plan to 2012.
3. Support executive team in accountability and alignment.
4. Complete Strategic Partnership objectives congruent with strategic plan.
5. Identify three key alliances.
6. Establish new investor strategy and ensure ABC is gaining investor support.
7. Gain Board alignment with strategy going forward.
8. Communicate clearly to all stakeholders.

Leadership Accountabilities:

I am personally accountable for:

1. Success of my direct reports through dialogue and coaching.
2. Company-wide focus on the strategy.
3. Ensure we maintain credibility with our customers.

Support Requirements:

I require the following support from:

Executive Team

1. Members support corporate strategy development thru respectful and honest dialogue.
2. Members articulate and meet their own accountabilities and goals.
3. Members work well as a team and focus on the success of the company as a whole.

Employees

1. Actively support the direction of ABC.
2. Deliver on your promises.
3. Share your accountability plan with your executive team and review all accountability plans as a team to ensure role clarity and to break down silos.
4. Cascade this approach to accountability plans down throughout the organization.

Figure 3:2 Sample CEO Accountability Plan. Adapted from Klatt, Murphy, and Irvine, *Accountability: Getting a Grip on Results,* Revised 2nd Edition (Bow River Publishing, 2003).

that switched to ROWE. The CEO learned of this initiative two years after it began transforming the company. He provided full support to keep the innovative initiative moving forward throughout the company.

There's a best practice from Best Buy. We're confident that you can do the same.

CHAPTER 4

Talent is More Than Pure Performance

We're Not Talking About Performing Seals

People perform at differing levels of effectiveness. The completion of tasks, no matter how mundane or quotidian, counts as performance. Seals perform quite nicely when they honk horns and balance balls on their noses, but few observers elbow their neighbor in the ribs and say, "What talent!"

Maya Angelou has pointed out that you train animals but you educate people. Organizations can be filled to the rafters with performers and still fail. World-class organizations require true talent.

WHAT IS TALENT AND WHY DOES IT MATTER?

What is talent? We believe you find it in someone with the *passion* and *competence* to meet a business need and *deliver results*—to meet or exceed the need.

Why does it matter? Because your talent pool is your competitive advantage given the worldwide shortage of true talent.

Definition of passion: You love what you do.

Alan once met a reporter from the New York Times. When he found out Alan was both a consultant and a psychologist, the reporter proceeded to lecture Alan on the fact that motivation is irrelevant, because he was demotivated by terrible hours, an autocratic editor, outdated equipment, and rowdy co-workers.

"Why don't you quit?" Alan asked.

"Are you crazy?" he yelled, "I love this work!"

Passion trumps pay. If it didn't, this would be a world without firefighters, teachers, nurses, and writers.

Passion is the number one critical success factor for top talent. If you have passion, you will develop the competence to meet a business need and deliver extraordinary results.

> **Talent Search**
>
> We consistently tell our executive coaching clients the same story: Hire enthusiasm and you can teach content. But if you hire content without enthusiasm, you'll never acquire talent.

We once sat on the recruiting committee with the CEO and executive team of a franchise business. The CEO engaged a recruiting company to assist him with hiring a rock-star VP-level sales executive to attract enough franchisees to achieve his high-growth strategy of doubling the number of stores in the next three years. The recruiting committee identified the top three candidates from the final list of 10. The top three candidates were asked to present a 90-day action plan to the CEO and executive team as a final step in the recruiting process.

The first two interviewees showed very little passion in their presentations. They both presented their understanding of the business need and their competence to deliver based on their previous experience. The third interviewee started the interview with, "I've been in the franchise business for 20 years, and I love this business. My father was in the franchise business for 40 years, and I plan to stay in this business forever. If you hire me, you'd better accelerate your high-growth plans because you'll have franchisees on a waiting list to invest in your business."

He got the job because he demonstrated the passion and competence to meet their business needs. A year later, he was recognized as the most valuable employee of the company.

Spend most of your time on passion and excellent activities and minimize your time on competent and incompetent activities to deliver extraordinary results; see the following descriptions.

Types of Activities:

Passion: extraordinary ability, energizes others
Excellent: excellent ability, little or no effect elsewhere
Competent: average ability, sometimes requires help
Incompetent: requires regular remedial help

With whom are you spending your time, energy, and development money?

Definition of competence: You have the skills, experience, and behaviors to deliver results.

Skills and experience are easy to define and develop in people. They are manifest in observed behavior. The biggest challenge in talent development is defining and developing success behaviors.

For example, tenured professors with poor student ratings have attended instructor development programs to learn teaching skills and they have many years of teaching experience. However, they don't have the success behaviors, such as connection, mood, and adaptability, to motivate and inspire students to learn. They have been rewarded entirely based on longevity and the ability to mark grades on papers. This is why you can observe tenured faculty—a prestigious distinction— who are virtually incompetent as teachers (the students do not learn the material).

Emotional intelligence has become a very effective tool in behavior management because it can be an effective tool to define, measure, and develop behaviors (a 27 percent predictor of job performance versus IQ, which is a 6 percent predictor).[1]

Emotional intelligence behaviors include self-awareness (self-confidence, mastering emotions, assertiveness, independence, life balance); interpersonal (empathy, connection); resilience (problem-solving, flexibility); stress management; and positive mood (happiness and optimism) (based on Bar-on tool).

Career derailment typically occurs due to a lack of self-awareness of the success behaviors required to influence the people around you.

Nancy had a 360 degree coaching assignment with the CFO of a large global publicly-held company. She interviewed board members, the CEO, his peers, and direct reports. The CFO was highly regarded by his boss, peers, and direct reports, but the

---

[1]Bar-on and Handley, *Optimizing People: A Practical Guide for Applying Emotional Intelligence to Improve Personal and Organizational Effectiveness* (Pro-Philes Press, 1999).

board had a very strong feeling that he was not the right CFO for the company.

She said to the CFO, "The board describes you as arrogant, dismissive, emotional, a poor listener, and not following through on board requests. They are not sure you are the right CFO for this company. What do you make of that?"

The CFO said, "I'm shocked. Most of them are idiots. They don't know our business, and they don't add any value. They ask stupid questions, and they give me a lot of work that doesn't make any sense to me so I don't do it."

Nancy replied, "Let's look at your emotional intelligence results. Which one of these behaviors are you missing when you show up at board meetings?"

He said, "Well, there are quite a few. I'm generally in a bad mood because I hate board meetings. I don't have a lot of empathy for them because I've never been on a board and, to be honest, I don't know what their role is. I guess I'm a bit too assertive when I push back at them. I guess I'm pretty judgmental when it comes to the board, and I'm embarrassed about it. I'm better than this, and it's time for me to change my behaviors."

Nancy coached the CFO to learn new behaviors of empathy and emotional self-awareness and to develop an action plan based on the feedback. The CFO attended a board meeting the following week and he completely shifted his behaviors. The CEO got several calls from board members after the board meeting to acknowledge the shift in attitude and behaviors of the CFO.

It really can be that simple.

Focus on leadership behaviors for succession planning. The higher up you go, the more emotional intelligence matters.

Another time Nancy facilitated a three-day succession planning workshop with the CEO and executive team of a large global company. Over the past three months I worked with the executive team to develop a three-year high-growth strategy.

The succession plan was now being developed to ensure that the company would have a strong leadership talent pool to execute the strategy.

Their leadership talent pool consisted of 120 people, and the goal of the succession plan was to identify and accelerate the development of the high potentials over the next three years aligned with the business strategy.

Nancy said, "Let's start with the COO. Is there anyone ready now with the right skills, experience, and behaviors to step into the COO role?"

The COO answered, "Absolutely not. We have one guy who might be ready in three years but he would have to have a complete overhaul." Everyone laughed. He said, "He has terrible people skills and we've had quite a few people leave because of him, but he's absolutely brilliant and he has more experience in operations than I do."

Nancy asked, "Does anyone in this room believe that an overhaul would lead to this guy being ready for the COO role within three years?" The VP of HR said, "To be honest, I think he is currently in the wrong role because he has no passion for leading people and his employee engagement scores are the lowest in the company. We need to move him to a technical specialist role before we lose even more people."

She told them, "One of the biggest mistakes companies make is putting people on succession plans who got promoted due to skills and experience without the focus on leadership behaviors."

Both of us often battle with clients who insist on ruining two jobs: promoting a great sales person to sales manager, or promoting a terrific CFO to COO. That's a magical way to lose two people at once. When I'm questioned about this, I simply point out the debacle of John Sculley going from Pepsi to Apple, and everyone is suddenly willing to listen.

Definition of delivering results: you deliver the specific agreed-upon results that you are accountable for (or you exceed them).

There is a big gap in talent management, a lack of focus on agreed-upon results and clarifying expectations. You can have passion and competence, but you need to focus on agreed-upon results to generate your ideal outcomes. People are putting in time doing activities, but they aren't focused on delivering agreed-upon results.

"We're in terrible shape since Joe retired," a general manager told Alan. "But Joe is sitting right there where he always does," Alan pointed out. "I didn't say he left," moaned the GM. "I just said that he retired."

Nancy was the executive coach to the newly appointed VP of business development of a large software company. The CEO hired the VP for her leadership and business development abilities. Before accepting the position, the VP clarified with the CEO that she was not a hands-on technical person. Nancy worked with the VP to develop her 90-day action plan to deliver very specific results. The CEO signed off on the results and action plan at the outset but, due to her travel schedule, her availability to coach and mentor her new VP was limited. After 90-days, the VP asked the CEO, "How am I doing? I've delivered all of the results that we agreed to, and I'm looking forward to making an even greater contribution in the future. Is there anything I can do to improve?"

The CEO said, "Your technical skills aren't very advanced, and I'm disappointed that you haven't learned our product." The VP resigned from the company within her first year. This is a typical example of lack of clarity on desired results, which leads to demoralized talent and retention issues.

We cited accountability plans as a requirement in Chapter 3. You must focus on employee-developed accountability plans versus job descriptions to accelerate business results and manage expectations. Job descriptions are static and focus on activities versus outcomes, a cardinal sin. Accountability plans are dynamic and empower employees to put in writing the results that they are accountable for.

As priorities change throughout the year, so do accountability plans and results.

THE DIFFERENCE BETWEEN GOOD AND OUTSTANDING

People who consistently exceed expectations over a long period of time (three-year minimum) are outstanding.

Outstanding people rarely know that they are outstanding.

We interviewed 10 board members as input to a 360 degree executive coaching program for an outstanding CEO of a large global company. The goal of the coaching program was for the CEO to raise the bar on his performance, and for him to be an exemplar to get everyone on his executive team to step up through participation in the 360 executive coaching program. He had been the CEO for more than eight years and every single board member described him as an outstanding CEO.

As a follow-up to the initial coaching assignment, we met with the board chair and the CEO to review the interview results and 90-day development plan. At the start of the meeting the board chair said, "Our CEO has exceeded our expectations every single year. He has led this company to become the world leader in our industry." The CEO said, "With all due respect, it was my world-class team that has made us the world leader of our industry. I've got my strengths, but as you can see from my 360 feedback results, I have lots of opportunities for development that I need to work on."

Outstanding people set high standards.

Nancy was the team coach to the newly appointed president of one of the divisions of a large financial institution. When he stepped into his new role, his division was ranked sixth out of the 10 divisions in the company.

His boss said, "You've taken on a huge challenge. This division has never been ranked higher than sixth, so if you can at least maintain a sixth ranking that would be a fantastic result."

The president said, "We can do better than sixth out of 10 if you'll support me in making some changes to my team. We'll get to at least a top three ranking this year, and we'll shoot for number one within three years."

His boss replied, "You sound like you have a big ego, and I think you'll burn out if you try." But the president said, "I love my job and I know what it takes to put a top team in place to deliver extraordinary results, so I'd like your support."

His division was ranked third in his first year, second in his second year, and first in his third year. He was promoted to a new role in his fourth year because he had the passion, competence, and focus on delivering extraordinary results.

Outstanding people aren't afraid to take risks.

Another time Nancy was the executive coach to the newly appointed EVP of HR of a large global company. In his former role, he was the CFO reporting to the CEO and he was listed on the succession plan as a potential CEO successor. The CEO had recently fired the EVP of HR for poor performance, and there were no ready-now internal candidates to step into the role.

The CEO said to the CFO, "I'd like you to consider taking the EVP HR role because we need to make HR strategic in this company. You have a 'ready now' successor and you have a lot of credibility on the executive team. I think you can learn the skills and gain the HR experience as you step into this new role."

The CFO said, "I'm the last person for this job. I'm a numbers guy. My wife is a VP HR for her company, but we don't talk shop at home! I'll do it, but we're both taking a big risk here."

The EVP HR was very successful in his new role, and he was promoted to president of a large division three years later.

> **Talent Search**
>
> As in sports, the "best available athlete" is more important than finding someone for a specific position who is limited to that role.

Outstanding people overcome barriers.

Again, Nancy acted as executive coach to a woman who was COO of a large financial institution. She had been reporting to her CEO for the past five years and she was listed on the CEO succession plan.

Nancy asked her, "Do you think you are ready now to take on the CEO role?" She said, "Yes, but there is a big barrier in the way."

"What's the big barrier?"

"Six months ago, I resigned because I couldn't put up with being bullied by our CEO anymore and that's what I told him. The CEO freaked out on me. Once he calmed down, he apologized and asked me to stay on. He said he would stop bullying me and my colleagues on the executive team in the future if I would stay on."

"If he has stopped his bullying behaviors, then you've just removed a big barrier for everyone, right?"

The board appointed her to the CEO position three years later.

Outstanding people park their egos.

Similarly, Nancy was executive coach to the VP Finance of a large global company. He had applied for the CFO role and he was one of two internal candidates applying for the job. He didn't get the CFO role, and the CEO was very concerned that he might leave the company. Nancy asked, "Are you planning to leave the company because you didn't get the CFO role?"

He said, "Absolutely not. I love this company and I think the CEO appointed a great CFO. I know there will be other great opportunities for me in this company. I plan to become the CEO of this company one day, so there will be other paths for me to get there from here."

In the Civil War, the Union was desperate for excellent generals, who were few and far between. After George Thomas won a great victory at Chickamauga covering a retreat and becoming known as The Rock of Chickamauga, he was offered command of the entire Army of the Tennessee. He refused, saying, "I'm not ready yet."

After a stunning victory at Nashville later, the only one in which an army was annihilated on the field (Hood's Army of Tennessee), he was offered the command again and accepted.

TALENT "OUTS"

We've always loved this term. Talent always emerges and beats nontalent, no matter how hard the latter tries, no matter how large the temporary lead, no matter how uneven the playing field.

Talent beats a focus on excuses.

Nancy facilitated a two-day retreat involving the president and executive team of a division of a large global company to develop a three-year high-growth strategy. As a final wrap-up to the session, the president asked each person on his 10-person executive team to commit to delivering on the agreed-upon strategy.

Everyone made a commitment to the president and the team, with the exception of one VP. The VP, who was accountable for 30 percent of the high-growth strategy, said, "I know we all want great success, but I just don't think we're being real about what we can achieve. Our industry is not doing very well and we have serious leadership talent shortages. Everyone is already working too hard, and I just don't think we're being realistic."

After working very closely with the VP over the next three months, the president offered him an early retirement package. A new VP was hired to put the right team in place to deliver on the high-growth strategy.

Alan worked with the general manager of a $600 million subsidiary for 90 days to convince him to fire the vice president of strategy who continually positioned himself as a victim of the competition, his incompetent peers, and the economy. Once that was finally done, the entire top team became dramatically more productive.

Talents beat those who are not committed to success.

Once Nancy was the executive coach to the CEO of a large global private company that had just been through a formal assessment from a potential acquiring company for the first time in the 40-year history of the company. Although an attractive offer was put forward, the owner of the company decided not to accept.

The CEO said, "The best thing about the due diligence process is I realized that I don't have the right team in place. As a result of the process, I fired my CFO and I think I have to fire my COO as well."

Nancy inquired, "What's the difference between the 'keepers' on your team and the people you are moving out of your team?"

He said, "The people I'm moving out of the team were not committed to the success of the team. During the due diligence process, they took personal holidays, they didn't deliver results, and they didn't honor many of the requests that were made of them." My 'keepers' were totally committed to the success of the team. We all gave up our personal time and made this our number one priority for six months to do the best we could to ensure success."

Talent Search

If you have to trust people—and you do—choose those who have exhibited the talent to make great calls and demonstrate outstanding instinct. Never trust the merely technically adept, and never, ever, the lawyers (who are fatally conservative).

Talent beats those who need protection.

Nancy was the executive coach to the CFO of a large global company. The results of the 360 degree feedback process indicated that board members, his boss, and peers all felt that the CFO was defensive about the people on his team.

She asked, "Are you aware that you get defensive when people give you feedback on your team members."

"Yes, I'm very defensive because they judge my team members too harshly and they don't see how hard everyone on my team is working."

"Top talent doesn't need you to protect them from being judged harshly. They are responsible for building their credibility and delivering results for the people around them. It's not about putting in time. It's about delivering results and managing expectations at all times."

Talent beats those who are in the wrong place at the wrong time.

Nancy delivered a two-day team effectiveness workshop for the CEO and executive team of a large global company. After the team session, the CEO approached Nancy and said, "I think I need to fire my CIO. I don't think he fits in well with the team. It was so obvious to me over the two days that people don't talk to him and they don't relate well to him. He's such a quiet guy, and the rest of us are all so passionate about the business and we love getting together as a team. His direct reports don't like him either, and I've been hearing a lot more noise about him over the past year."

"He's been on your team for three years, and the situation is not getting any better. Everyone is put on the planet to achieve their full potential. He's likely in the wrong place at the wrong time."

The following week, the CIO handed in his resignation and let the CEO know that he would be joining a much smaller company that would enable him to be a lot more hands-on with technology.

ASSESSING YOUR RESOURCES: THE TALENT TEST

The critical success factor in attracting, developing, and retaining top talent is an assessment approach that helps people achieve their full potential.

Assessment involves ongoing feedback throughout the year: Quarterly performance reviews with all direct reports are recommended and, when done properly, there are no surprises during performance reviews. These need to be based on agreed-upon outcomes and measures of success.

This is Jack Welch's best practices differentiation model:

A players—exceed expectations (20 percent)

B players—meet expectations (70 percent)

C players—do not meet expectations (10 percent)

Five main approaches to assessing talent

1. *Self-assessment*

Listen first to self-assessments.

Nancy was the executive coach to the chair of the board of a private company. The chair said, "I have to do the CEO annual performance review next week and I'm a bit concerned."

"What concerns you?"

"I have to deliver some tough messages about delivering results and he's not going to like it."

"Ask him to do a self-evaluation and listen first before you give him any feedback. If his assessment and your assessment are aligned, then coach him on how to deliver greater results. If his assessment is worse than your assessment, give him feedback to rebuild his self-confidence. If his assessment is better than your assessment, then have a candid conversation about the different points of view. Once you reach agreement on the assessment, develop an action plan to prevent this situation from happening again."

Self-assessment is the most empowering approach to performance management if outcomes are clearly defined and ongoing feedback is provided in a timely manner.

2. *Peer assessment*

Include peer feedback as input.

Nancy was facilitating one of her CEO forums involving 14 CEOs of large companies and she said, "If you want to break down silos, you need to include peer feedback for performance reviews."

One of the CEOs said, "I've decided to get peer feedback once a year for each of my direct reports. In order to ensure

71

candor and confidentiality, I ask them to call my confidential voicemail and give me feedback on what's working and what needs improvement for each of their peers. I started using this approach three years ago. I tie the qualitative results to their bonus, and the behavior change has been outstanding."

Companies need to develop better approaches to foster trust and candor so that valuable peer feedback is provided on an ongoing basis. For example, I delivered a two-day team building session for the CEO and executive team of a large global software company. There were 10 people on the team and, as part of the team building session, each person was asked to provide feedback on "one strength and one opportunity for development" for each member of the team including the CEO. This exercise significantly increased trust and candor on the team. As a result, the CEO and his team have been doing this exercise without external support on a quarterly basis.

3. *Direct report assessment*

Include direct report feedback as input starting with the CEO.

When Stephen Kaufman was the CEO at Arrow Electronics, he initiated a formal process for getting performance feedback from his board of directors, which included board members getting feedback from his direct reports on five key areas: leadership, strategy, people management, operating metrics, and external relationships (see Harvard Business Review article, October 2008, "Evaluating the CEO," by Stephen Kaufman). Cascading this approach to getting feedback from direct reports for all leaders as input to performance reviews is a very effective approach to accelerating performance.

4. *Boss assessment*

Focus on strengths. Then identify opportunities for development.

Nancy worked as the executive coach to the regional VP of a large retail company. Over the past year, this woman had been reporting to the COO and she had just completed her first annual performance review with him.

She said, "Nancy, I think I have to quit my job. My region is ranked number one out of eight regions in our company and my COO spent the entire one-hour review telling me about all the things I'm doing wrong. I'm just not motivated to work with him."

Nancy said, "Focus on your strengths and don't let one person's opinion—even though he is your boss—stop you from making the biggest contribution you can to your company."

Three months later the COO was fired and Nancy's client was promoted to COO. People don't leave companies—they leave bosses. Focus on strengths during performance reviews and provide ongoing feedback to avoid surprises.

Talent Search

If individual results aren't being measured and communicated informally and formally on a frequent basis, you have no idea of where your talent resides or if you're even using it effectively.

---

5. *External assessment*

Invest in external assessments for top talent and succession planning.

The CEO of a large global company decided to hire an external assessment company to do psychological testing of all succession candidates. Nancy was the executive coach to the president of a division of a large global company who was listed on the company succession plan. The president was asked to attend a one-day assessment session with a registered psychologist. Nancy said to him, "Let's come up with an action plan to prepare for the one-day session."

He said, "I need an action plan for this?"

"If you want to stay on the succession plan, you need to be prepared and familiar with the process to ensure success.

Find out more about the assessment company. Ask your boss if she or anyone in her circle has been through this process. Talk to HR about the implications of the results. Practice doing some online IQ and emotional intelligence tests."

Nancy debriefed with the president after the one-day assessment session and he said, "I did really well on the test results because I was calm and prepared. I scored in the 80th percentile on one of the tests because I was familiar with IQ and emotional intelligence tests. I'm more confident now than ever that I will have many great promotion opportunities with this company so I plan to stay for a very long time."

Never allow yourself to confuse performance with talent. Your HR department is probably training people more than educating them. You must put a halt to this, and begin to identify and develop true talent.

If you want trained seals, go to the circus.

CHAPTER 5

The Semi-Renewable Resource

You Can Replant Trees, but Talent Doesn't Grow so Easily

When a tree decays it is not normally from sickness and never (one assumes) from sin. It decays because it has reached its maximum growth maintaining that size and weight for the period usual with that type of tree. It cannot live forever in any case. Institutions, whether political or industrial, are not essentially different.

—Professor C. Northcote Parkinson,
In-Laws and Outlaws

IF TALENT WERE READILY RENEWABLE, EVERY COMPANY WOULD BE EXCELLENT

Excellent companies create talent by developing people strategies that are aligned with the business strategy.

People Strategy Key Objective: The availability of top talent to deliver results required by the business strategy. See Table 5.1, Sample One-Page Company Strategy; it includes key people strategies.

Key People Strategies

1. *What is the culture (values) we need to achieve better performance in our measures of competitive advantage (industry critical success factors)? How do we want people to behave in the future so that we get better results than we do today? For high-growth companies, the value of innovation is critical to accelerating business results.*

Nancy was the team coach to the Innovation Team of a high-growth company in the retail industry. A year ago, the CEO decided to set up a cross-functional Innovation Team consisting of high potentials in the company who would make recommendations to the executive team. In Nancy's first meeting with the Innovation Team she asked, "Has your team been able to make progress in shifting the company to a culture of innovation?" They said, no, this team has been a waste of our time because the executive team doesn't approve any of our recommendations. They just want to keep doing things the same way.

Nancy asked, "What if your recommendations went to the CEO for approval instead of the entire executive team? Would this approach speed up innovation?" The team leader and Nancy met with the CEO the following week and he agreed to make all future decisions based on recommendations from the Innovation Team. The CEO got some resistance from his executive team, but he was able to achieve his goal of shifting to an innovation culture by doing things differently himself.

Table 5.1   Sample One-Page Company Strategy

Culture and Values:
Results-Driven Innovation Customer First
3–5 Year Vision and Mission:
Vision: To be the best company in Western Canada in our industry. *Mission:* We build luxury homes to help people in NA enjoy their lives more fully.
Customer Value Proposition:
What strategy will you use to beat the competition? *Best cost:* Are you the Wal-Mart of your industry? *Customer Service:* Are you the BMW of your industry? *Innovation:* Are you the Sony of your industry? Customer Value Proposition: We are the BMW of our industry.
Scorecard:
Customer Satisfaction Objectives and Strategies:
Objectives: 100 percent Customer Satisfaction *Strategies:* Implement Customer Loyalty Program
People Objectives and Strategies:
Objectives: To be recognized as a "Best Place to Work" in Canada by 2010. *Strategies:* Implement succession management and leadership development program. Identify and develop people strategies for strategic job functions. Develop and implement a new performance management and compensation system.
Operational Effectiveness Objectives and Strategies:
Objectives: Reduce supplier management costs by 20 percent. *Strategies:* Business Process Innovation ERP Implementation
Financial Objectives and Strategies:
Objectives: Double in size (revenues) by 2010. *Strategies:* 50 percent expansion with existing customers 50 percent new customer acquisition

2. Identify strategic job families that have the greatest impact on the strategy, based on internal processes.

Research studies (see Kaplan and Norton, *Strategy Maps: Converting Intangible Assets into Tangible Outcomes*, Harvard Business School, 2004) indicate that the success of the company strategy is determined by how well the company develops competencies in less than 10 percent of the workforce.

Alan worked with Merck to develop talent recruitment processes that were sometimes called heroic because of the lengths the company went to secure top talent. However, we had to discriminate as to where it was really needed. At the time, it was in bench chemists, and a certain specialty among bench chemists. Those people were key in the then-current strategy of Merck, but other job classifications were not.

Nancy worked with the executive team of a transportation company to develop a people strategy to accelerate business results. The company had 1,200 employees (75 percent union). The CEO decided to hold an urgent two-day people strategy session because the company had just been through a very difficult union negotiation (involving significant work disruption) that had resulted in the loss of the company's biggest customer account, resulting in significant lay-offs. At the start of the people strategy session, Nancy asked, "What's the 10 percent of your workforce that has the greatest impact on your ability to execute your strategy?" The VP HR said, "We have 75 supervisors of union staff, and if we don't focus on attracting, retaining, and developing our supervisors we'll be out of business." Everyone agreed, so most of the time together was spent developing people strategies for the strategic job family of supervisors.

3. Leadership development and succession planning.

The availability of qualified leaders at all levels is needed to deliver results. Common leadership development approaches

79

include programs in the areas of internal coaching and mentoring, job shadowing, executive coaching, and internal and external executive education programs.

Nancy met with the CEO of a large global company to define the objectives of a people strategy project. The CEO said, "We don't have to worry about succession planning and leadership development because it's all done and the board has approved our plan. We have our top-20 list of high potentials so we're all set."

Nancy asked, "Based on your high-growth strategy, have you identified what the company will look like three years from now from a leadership perspective? For example, how many presidents and VPs and directors will you need to run the company when you've doubled in size? Do you have any idea of what the leadership gaps will be?"

He said, "No, but it'll be a lot more than the top-20 list of high potentials that we have today." The CEO did the leadership gap analysis and presented it to the executive team at the people strategy session. The shocked looks created a sense of urgency to accelerate the development of internal succession candidates and expedite the hiring of external talent to fill the gaps.

4. *People management.*

Strategies to attract, retain, and develop top talent at all levels of the organization. See Chapter 2: The five failings.

5. *Performance management and compensation.*

Alignment of goals and incentives with the strategy. See Chapter 4: Assessing your resources: The talent test.

Talent Search

Talent has to be nurtured, so you need an organization of nurturers among the leadership team. If talent dies, find out what life support was missing and why.

---

6. Organization structure and role clarity.

Strategy drives structure and role clarity to ensure that all employees are strategically focused and to avoid role conflict.

Restructuring is very stressful and disruptive to everyone involved so it must be done properly; whenever you change reporting relationships, it's like breaking up a team (and sometimes more like a marriage!). It takes time for people to build new reporting relationships and to let go of old ones.

It's not about moving people and boxes; it's about putting a structure in place to accelerate strategy execution. Role clarity is very critical to getting everyone set up for success.

Nancy was the executive coach to the CEO of a large insurance company. The CEO had 18 direct reports, and she had just hired an external COO and moved four of her direct reports under the COO. She asked, "What can I do to minimize the disruption to my team? I don't want people to leave because they didn't get promoted and they don't get to report to me anymore."

Nancy replied, "Strategy drives structure and role clarity. Bring the entire executive team (including the new COO) together and review your strategy. Explain what the new COO will be responsible and accountable for and what you will be letting go of as a result of the restructuring. Explain why you are making the change now and relate it back to the strategy. Maintain close relationships with everyone on your senior leadership team, not just your direct reports, in order to retain top talent."

The CEO didn't lose any of her top talent, but it took about three months for her former direct reports to stop going to her directly with key issues and challenges (even though she directed them back to the COO every time).

Once we worked with an optical products company that had a new division president. There was some awkwardness among the senior team, even though the predecessor wasn't

81

particularly admired. But we found out that he did permit a more freewheeling executive council meeting.

"Don't try to prove yourself," we advised the new president. "Let them enjoy their comfortable camaraderie." It turned out that was easier for everyone, and the team soon slipped into a great working relationship.

7. *Teamwork.*

Sharing of knowledge and eliminating functional silos and bureaucracy to enable strategy execution.

Teamwork starts at the top; if the executive team works in silos, so does everyone else in the company. The CEO must hold people accountable and reward team behavior to break down silos.

Another time we worked with the executive team of a large restaurant chain to improve team effectiveness. The CEO wanted to break down the silos between all of the functional areas in order to speed up strategy execution. At the first team session the CEO said, "I fired our former COO three months ago because I knew he would never let go of his silo mind-set. We're here today because we need to work as a team and breakdown the silos."

We spent the entire day reviewing and defining each executive team member's accountability plan and in particular the interdependencies between roles (see Chapter 3, Strategy execution: Creating a culture of accountability for results). At the end of the session the new COO said, "I've never had this level of open dialogue about roles in my entire career. I really feel set up for success in my new role now that we've all committed to helping each other be successful."

Be careful: Many companies successfully work with committees, not teams. A team wins or loses together. A committee collaborates, but individual members may be more successful than others. Determine which structures you ideally need and what the talent requirements are.

8. *Internal communications.*

Once the people strategy is developed, it must be communicated to 360 degree stakeholders (board, leadership, all employees).

Internal Communications Strategies:

a. Define internal stakeholder objectives in terms of behavior change, which will lead to accelerated business results.

Example: Every employee in the company:
- understands and accepts the people strategy
- understands how his or her role contributes to the success of the people strategy
- becomes strategically focused

b. Prioritize stakeholders based on their impact on people strategy execution. Use a cascading approach to communication whereby every leader in the organization is responsible and accountable for communicating the people strategy to all direct reports.

Example:
- Engage NOW: Executive team
- Engage NOW: Top management team
- Inform NOW: All employees

c. Define communication channels based on reach, effectiveness, consistency, interactivity, and timing. The most cost-effective way to expedite strategy execution is to maximize the use of face-to-face communication strategies (workshops, meetings, teleconferences, presentations, newsletters, intranet).

d. Prepare messages to create a sense of urgency for everyone in the company to become people-focused.

- Why do we need to change?
- Where are we going and what will the future look like?

- How will we get there?
- Who will be leading us into the future?
- When will change happen?
- What's in it for me?

e. Develop a people strategy communication plan.

- Identify stakeholder categories
- Prepare messages
- Identify channels
- Identify timeframe
- Identify lead person for planning
- Identify lead person for communication
- Get feedback and measure whether objectives were achieved

f. Commit to CEO and executive team accountability for the results of the people strategy communication plan.

TREES DON'T MOVE, TALENT DOES

Why does talent move?

1. *Lack of job satisfaction needs being met*

People leave when one or more of their job satisfaction needs are not being met (see the following list of the top six job satisfaction needs).

- Connection to boss is the key retention strategy. People leave bosses not companies. Just like people leave spouses, not families or lifestyle.
- Build trust and candor in reporting relationships to ensure that current and future roles will meet job satisfaction needs.

Nancy was the executive coach to the president of a major division of a large manufacturing company. The president had been with the company for seven years and he was thinking about resigning because he felt that he was losing his passion for his job.

At the first coaching session Nancy asked, "On a scale of 1(low) to 10 (high), how would you rate your current job in terms of meeting your needs in these top six job satisfaction areas?" His ratings and responses are below. He resigned six months later. The CEO was shocked by his resignation. If you don't like surprises, build trust and candor with your reporting relationships in order to retain top talent.

Six human needs for job satisfaction:

(Source: Anthony Robbins, *Get the Edge*, personal journal)

1. Love/connection: 4/10 "I don't really like many of the guys on the executive team so I don't feel much connection."
2. Contribution: 4/10 "I don't think I'm making a big contribution to my team's success. I have a great team in place that could run the business without me."
3. Significance: 3/10 "It doesn't matter how well we do, I never get acknowledged by our CEO. I get paid a lot, but nothing is ever good enough for him."
4. Learning and growth: 3/10 "I'm not learning anything new."
5. Certainty: 2/10 "I don't get along very well with the CEO. He's a control freak, and we're always butting heads, so who knows if I'll get fired."
6. Variety: 2/10: "I've been in this role for seven years so it's very predictable."

2. *Generation Clashes*

- In most companies, top positions are held by boomers.
- In order to minimize generation clashes (see descriptions below), boomers need to realize that Gen X and Gen Y

have different expectations, particularly in the areas of (1) life balance; (2) a career plan involving more than one company; and (3) technology.

- New people strategies need to be developed to address the needs of each generation.

Descriptions of Workforce Generations:

Boomers (age 44–62): Loyalty to one company; "work-first" mindset; can be uncomfortable with technology.

Generation X (age 32–43): Move around; "life balance" mindset; utilize technology.

Generation Y (age 31 and under): Move around; "life balance" mindset; love technology.

3. *Life Balance Clash*

Nancy worked with the executive team of a North American retail company that was having great difficulty retaining top talent at all levels of the company, except the top level. The CEO said, "I'm 62 years old, and most of us on our executive team did not grow up with life balance. We know that the new generations want it, so we need your help with coming up with some new retention strategies."

Over the next three months she worked with the executive team to put in place some new strategies, including a four-day work week strategy for everyone in the company, which they implemented immediately. Later, Nancy asked the sales executive, "How's the four-day work week working for you?"

He said, "It's a real problem. I'm 40 years old, and I have a wife and three kids. I've been with the company for 10 years, and I moved to a four-day work week because I thought it was a great way for me to finally achieve life balance in this company. My CEO is not coping very well. He said he might have to fire me if he can't reach me on Fridays." The sales executive resigned three months later and went to the competition, who hired him on a four-day work week and doubled his vacation time. Now more than ever, Gen X top talent has options, and culture clashes get in the way of retention.

> **Talent Search**
>
> Don't "project," which is the psychological phenomenon of assuming others want what you want, are motivated by what motivates you, and fear what you fear. Cross-generationally, that's a guarantee of a breakdown in understanding.

4. *Technology Clash*

Nancy was the executive coach to the COO of a large global retail company. He was also responsible for the IT function of his company. He said, "I really hate running IT for our company. Over the past six months, we've lost five of our IT people to the competition and I don't know why. We keep throwing more money at them and they still keep leaving."

Nancy asked, "How old are the people who left?"

He said, "mid to late 20s."

She suggested, "Find out what technology the competition is using and you'll know why." Gen Ys—not just IT people who are Gen Ys—love technology and expect to have access to current technology to do their jobs."

5. *Career Plan Clash*

Once Nancy was reviewing the CEO succession plan with the CEO of a large global company who was going to retire within 12 months. The CEO said, "I have four great candidates that I'm grooming for my position, but I already know who the board should pick. There is only one guy on my team who has been with this company his whole career, and loyalty is more important than anything when it comes to CEO succession."

Nancy's question was, "Is he a great strategic thinker and does he have great people skills?"

He said, "He's got younger guys on the team who can help him with those areas." The board selected the CEO's top pick for the position and all three other candidates left within three months.

6. *Male Filters*

Another time Nancy was the executive coach to a woman who was CFO of a large financial institution. She wanted to become "CEO ready-now" and her CEO indicated to her that he would be retiring within two years. As input to her 360 degree executive coaching program, Nancy interviewed 12 board members to get feedback on the CFO's strengths and opportunities for development. Four of 12 board members provided feedback that "she should not become the CEO because she has young kids and it's just not proper for a young female to become the CEO." During the first coaching session Nancy asked the CFO, "How old are your kids?" She said, "They are both in university." Nancy told her, "Bring a family photo to your next board meeting and you might be considered for the CEO job." Retaining top female talent requires awareness of male filters that get in the way of assessing top talent.

TALENT ISN'T FOREVER—IT CAN OBSOLESCE

Talent has a shelf life in most cases. Four key areas where talent can obsolesce:

1. *IT Talent*

We worked on strategy development with the executive team of a high-growth company in the auto industry. During the pre-work analysis, everyone identified lack of IT systems to enable growth as one of the top three weaknesses of the company. At the first strategy session, the CIO said, "I strongly disagree with listing lack of IT systems as a weakness. You people don't understand anything about technology and my team works really hard to develop all of our systems in-house."

The CFO said, "I think we need to move into the 21st-century and buy some software packages so we can speed up getting technology to enable our business growth." After the strategy session, the CEO realized that the CIO had spent his entire career developing software and he was not going to make the transition to using software packages. Three months later, he brought in a new CIO with software package experience to develop and execute an IT strategy to enable business growth.

2. *Blocker Talent*

Nancy was the executive coach to the newly appointed president of a major division of a large global company. The president was brought in to accelerate business results. At the first coaching session he said, "I think this is going to be a real challenge. My right-hand guy (second in command) applied for my job and didn't get it. He's been with the company for over 30 years. He's three years away from retirement, and according to everyone on the team he doesn't deliver results. My CEO says I have to keep him on the team for political reasons."

Nancy suggested, "Ask him what he loves to do and create a role for him that gives him lots of autonomy (with no reporting relationships) so he can continue to contribute until he retires without getting in the way of progress for everyone else. Move blocker talent out of the way."

> **Talent Search**
>
> In shuffleboard, bocci, and curling, teams use a blocking technique to prevent opponents from scoring. Don't allow your own organization to create talent blockers that prevent you from reaching your strategic goals.

3. *No Passion Talent*

Nancy delivered a two-day leadership development retreat for the executive team of a high-growth global company. At the end of the two-day retreat, one of the company presidents said to her in private, "I have to quit my job. I've been with this company for 20 years, and I'm listed on the CEO succession plan. I've lost my passion and I know I need to quit my job and get on with my life. This has been going on for about a year. I'm just not excited about work anymore, and I'm having a hard time showing up for work every day."

Nancy's reply was, "Passion is more important than anything else when it comes to delivering results. It's pretty obvious to everyone else that you've lost your passion, so go talk to your CEO *now* and move on with your life."

4. *Overwhelm Talent*

One of Nancy's CEO clients was planning a six-month sabbatical with his family. He was grooming his COO to become the acting CEO while he was away for the six months. About two months before his sabbatical, Nancy got a call from her client.

He said, "Nancy, I can't leave my COO in charge while I'm away. He's just gone on long-term medical leave due to stress and depression."

She asked, "Had he been showing signs of stress?"

He said, "Yes, but that's normal given the circumstances. We've all been through the merger together, and we've all been working really long hours."

The CEO had to cancel his sabbatical. If the person in charge can't handle the stress, then perhaps he isn't the right fit for an expanded role.

THE LAST THING YOU NEED IS PARITY

You want all-stars who stand out. Egalitarianism ruins teams, ruins politics, and can ruin your organization. You want the best to stand out because they will propel you forward. Business is not about giving everyone a chance.

If everyone is alike, then you probably have mediocrity.

We delivered a three-day leadership development and succession planning program for the executive team of a large manufacturing company. The CEO kicked off the session and said, "We're here today because our board thinks we're too internally focused and that we need a more diverse executive and overall leadership talent pool." During the round of introductions, we learned that all of the guys on the executive team had been accountants from the same accounting firm—even the HR guy!

Talent Search

It's tough to make these calls, but the leader has to identify, isolate, and support those who are the true all-stars. Talent is a rare resource, and you must take steps to preserve and protect it.

All-stars ruffle feathers and deliver results.

We delivered a two-day team effectiveness program for the top team of a large professional services firm. Before the program we interviewed all 15 participants to learn more about the team strengths and opportunities for improvement. One key theme that emerged was that the new partner, who had just joined the team six months ago, wasn't fitting in well with everyone else on the team because his results in his first six months were making them all look bad.

All-stars want flexibility, so give it to them.

Nancy once coached the CFO of a large global company who had been with the company for over five years and had delivered extraordinary results. He quickly became the CEO's right-hand person even though others had been on the executive team for much longer. As input to the coaching assignment, she interviewed all board members, his peers, and his direct reports. One key theme that emerged from the peer feedback was that the CFO wasn't very loyal to the company because he did not move to the head office where all the other executives lived. Be flexible if you want to attract top talent. It's worth it.

All-stars have the courage to make change happen.

Another time we coached the newly appointed COO of a large construction company. The COO had been with the company for just over six months and he was hired to help turn the company around. In order to do so, he replaced all of the existing management team members with people who had worked with him in his previous company. And, the productivity of the workforce had increased by 30 percent since he joined the company. The COO felt that although his approach was not supported by his peers, he had the support of the CEO, which gave him the courage to keep moving forward to make change happen.

If you agree that talent is a scarce and only semi-renewable resource, then you're probably interested in where you can best go, and how you can best act, to harvest it.

CHAPTER 6

Talent Is Attracted, Not Recruited

The Myths of Corporate Recruiting

Corporate recruiting is often somewhere between mind-numbing matrices and a set of Tarot cards. Everyone provides lip service about its importance, but no one wants to engage in it as a central executive accountability.

We're going to explore some of the myths and realities from our experience.

COMPETING BY DOLLARS IS SILLY AND EXPENSIVE

Pay and benefits don't win the attraction game. Let's say that in a different way: Pay and benefits don't win the attraction game.

Buckingham and Coffman, in *First Break All the Rules* (1999), developed the following set of 12 questions to measure the core elements needed to attract, focus, and retain the most talented employees.

Notice there are no questions dealing with pay or benefits. The results of their study showed that pay and benefits were equally important to every employee, good, bad, or mediocre. If you are 20 percent below the market average, you may have difficulty attracting people. If your pay and benefits packages are up to market levels, you're in the game but it's not going to help you win.

> **Talent Search**
> If you provide mediocre people with better pay and benefits, you have wealthier, better cared for mediocre people.

Here are the 12 factors:

1. Do I know what is expected of me at work?
2. Do I have the materials and equipment I need to do my work right?
3. At work, do I have the opportunity to do what I do best every day?

4. In the last seven days, have I received recognition or praise for doing good work?

5. Does my supervisor, or someone at work, seem to care about me as a person?

6. Is there someone at work who encourages my development?

7. At work, do my opinions seem to count?

8. Does the mission/purpose of my company make me feel my job is important?

9. Are my co-workers committed to doing quality work?

10. Do I have a best friend at work?

11. In the last six months, has someone at work talked to me about my progress?

12. This last year, have I had opportunities at work to learn and grow?

Great bosses win the attraction game

There are a lot of lists of "Top 100 Best, Super, Fabulous Places to Work" (for Gen X, for minorities, for women, for boomers, for goof-offs) based on criteria such as on-site day care, vacation time, profit sharing, spas, aromatherapy, parking privileges, Zodiac sign, and training programs. These are all important to someone, we suppose, *but the criterion of "great bosses" is more important than anything else.*

Nancy was the executive coach to the newly appointed CFO of a large forestry company. She asked him, "The forestry industry is the worst it's ever been and this company might not survive. It'll be quite some time before you ever see a bonus. Why did you join this company?"

He said, "Our CEO has the best track record and reputation in the industry. I know that I'll learn a lot from him. I got this job because the former CFO retired. Everyone else on the executive team has been with our CEO for over 15 years. People stay with great bosses, and I'm glad I joined a winning team."

Alan once asked someone at JPMorgan Chase why he continued to work for an overpowering boss who held everyone to extremely high standards and was uncompromising on performance.

"Because he's a winner," the man said, "and we're all learning. After succeeding working for him, we'll all succeed anywhere in the firm."

As they say about New York, "If you can make it there, you can make it anywhere."

Bad bosses will always lose the attraction and retention game.

So much money has been thrown at the challenge of attracting and retaining top talent in the form of better pay and better perks. However, attraction and retention are mostly a leadership issue. If you have an attraction and retention problem, look first to your leaders. It is the relationship with his/her immediate boss that will determine how long an employee stays and how productive he/she is while with the company.

Nancy was the executive coach to a newly appointed woman COO of a large health care organization. Nancy asked her, "What made you decide to join this organization?" She said, "I joined this organization because I had worked with Joe previously and he's a great boss. Joe is the EVP, and I don't have to report to the CEO. She has a terrible reputation, and I would not want to report to her." Six months later, Joe and two other people resigned from the executive team. The CEO offered the COO a promotion to Joe's EVP role and she declined. The COO left shortly after.

Alan was the executive coach to the VP HR of a large retail company. The VP HR had been with the company for only nine months and she was considering leaving the company. Alan asked her, "This is a great company with a great brand, why do you want to leave?"

She said, "My first boss just got fired, and my new 'acting' boss doesn't know anything about HR. I told my new 'acting' boss during our first meeting that I took this job because my former boss indicated that I would be on the succession plan to take over her role. My new 'acting' boss said he was 99 percent sure that would never happen and that they would be going externally for her replacement." Alan instructed, "Go talk to your CEO about your situation and if he doesn't get it then leave." Fortunately, the CEO stepped in and the VP HR got promoted to EVP and stayed with the company.

Here is an informal list of the traits among bosses that cause people to be attracted and to stay. Remember, most people leave their boss, not their job, and certainly not their career, when they depart from a company.

- Accessibility: Good bosses don't disappear when traveling (they answer e-mail and phone messages), nor during a crisis, nor during the normal day.
- Balance: They don't allow a personal concern, no matter how severe, to change their leadership regimen or treatment of others.
- Consistency: We've found unequivocally that people require consistency in their leadership so that they can make reasonable judgments and assumptions about what to expect.
- Unanticipated feedback: They don't wait until formal meetings to provide constructive feedback, which may be positive or negative but is always aimed at improvement.
- Opportunity to exercise talent: Outstanding leaders don't simply adhere to job descriptions (most can't even lay their hands on them). They continually provide challenge and "stretch" for subordinates.
- Freedom to fail: Failure is never fatal, although failing consistently due to the same cause or unlearned lesson probably will be.
- Empathy: They may not feel what you feel, not even agree with it, but they understand it enough to be empathic when required.

Jack Welch, Lee Iacocca, Henry Ford, Steve Jobs, Bill Gates, Rudy Giuliani, Andrea Jung, and scores of others have been cited as notoriously difficult to work for by people who did everything they could to keep working with them. That's because they are and were outstanding leaders whom people sought to follow and learn from, but they were not out to win popularity contests. When Jack Welch fielded unvetted questions in the famous "pit" at GE's training facility at Crotonville, New York, it was highly inspirational (which is why about 50 times the actual number of people who were there for these sessions claim to have been there).

WHY "MOST DESIRED" LISTS DON'T MATTER

Recruiting is like the dating game. If you know what you're looking for, you're likely to find it within your desired time frame. If you don't, then you'll spend a lot of time and money playing the game with unsatisfactory results. (And speed recruiting is about as satisfactory as speed dating.)

Hire for culture fit versus skills and experience

Nancy was the coach for the executive team of a large global transportation company. The CEO fired the CIO, who had been with the company for less than a year. The CEO asked Nancy, "Do you think I did the right thing? The CIO didn't get along with his peers and I got a lot of complaints about him from his team. I knew when I hired him that he might not be a fit for our culture, but I needed someone with strong technical skills to help us get a handle on our IT function. He had great technical skills but he just didn't fit the culture."

Nancy asked, "What did you learn from that experience?"

He said, "Cultural fit trumps skills and experience every time."

Here is an example of a set of desired cultural traits for a company:

- We have honesty and integrity as our number one value.
- We grow our business.

99

- We pay for performance.
- We have fun.
- We face tough issues.

A set of behavioral interviews can be developed for these traits to use during the recruiting process. Now, more than ever, companies are going beyond behavioral interviews and dinners with spouses to ensure cultural fit. For example, Wal-Mart hires actors to perform during the recruiting process. Potential hires show up on the job for a day (as if they've been hired) and work (with actors) to deliver results.

By the way, the bullet points above reflect the generic lists that so many companies wind up with, despite the length of the retreat they sponsor to achieve them. (They might as well do it by e-mail and save the money.)

Here are some cultural traits we've compiled from more original and sophisticated clients:

- We challenge each other openly and constructively.
- We engage our customers and suppliers in decisions that affect them.
- We encourage employees to spend 20 percent of their time on corporate issues of interest to them, irrespective of their job descriptions.
- We intend to earn 25 percent of our profits from products and services that didn't exist five years ago.
- Our intent is to thrive and grow, even in poor economic climates.

Spend more time recruiting and less time firing

Nancy was the executive coach to the newly appointed COO of a large global technology company. He said, "I can't believe how insane the recruiting process is for this company. I had to go through 18 interviews and it took over six months to get hired. I met more than 50 senior people in the company. I don't know how I'm ever going to get the right people on my team if it takes so long to make things happen."

Nancy commented, "You probably already have the right people on your team, given your recruiting process."

We've found that the key to recruiting is to make it a leadership function, with peripheral groups such as human resources merely checking for basic criteria and basic vetting (e.g., validating college transcripts, following up on references).

> **Talent Search**
>
> Make recruiting and retention an important aspect of senior executives' bonus calculations, with clear measures of success, and watch the organization improve overnight.

Partner with recruiters

Now more than ever, you need to partner with recruiters to help you define the traits that are most important to you in employees and to attract top talent.

Many of our CEO clients have been getting frustrated with recruiting companies because they aren't able to find top talent fast enough given the war for talent. Nancy is the executive coach and facilitator of six CEO networks consisting of over 80 CEOs. One of my CEO clients in one of my CEO forums shared with his peers, "We got so frustrated with recruiters that we decided to do our own search for one of our key positions. We spent $50,000 advertising for one of our key positions and we only got three resumes. We'll never do that again."

She also was the executive coach to a very successful entrepreneurial CEO who owned many successful companies across a wide variety of industries. He had been searching for a potential successor for more than a year with no success. He said, "I started out thinking I wanted an entrepreneur just like me, but I haven't found that person."

Nancy asked, "Have you defined the traits that are most important to you given the role you would like that person to play?"

He said, "It's all in my head and I'll know it when I see it." I introduced him to a recruiter who helped him develop a "most desired traits" list and within three months he hired his successor.

Every leader should find a few recruiters whom they can really trust and rely upon. But this is a partnership, not an abdication. Executives and recruiters with close professional ties and similar values find better talent more quickly.

Partner with your HR function

We completed a succession plan and leadership development program with the executive team of a large manufacturing company. Some immediate needs for hiring people into key positions were identified during the project.

We followed up with the VP HR a week later to see if any progress had been made and she said, "I'm waiting to hear back from the president of that division. He's supposed to tell me his requirements for the key position and then I can start the recruiting process." We asked her, "Isn't that something you could help him with? You could help speed up the recruiting, which will accelerate business results." Be proactive and form a partnership with your HR function that involves more than just order taking.

But allow HR to check for the "musts" that are obvious, such as industry experience or a track record of success, while key front line leaders assume the responsibility for the nuances, the chemistry, and the tough challenges.

MAXIMIZING APPLICATION OF TALENT DRIVES UP ATTRACTION

The more people exercise their talents on the job, the more they feel motivated, and the more people will be attracted who want to exercise their talents. It's fine for people to engage in their talents off the job but, ideally, you want to fully engage people so that they can't wait to apply something even after hours, rather than rush to go home at five so that they can apply something that can't be used on the job.

We've watched vital people become heavily engaged in the community, serving on local boards, coaching Little League, running fundraisers, even seeking political office, because all of those leadership and organizational skills had no outlet at work. We're not advocating workaholics, but we are suggesting that if someone has a talent, everyone is better off if it can be expressed at work (which is not mutually exclusive to also expressing it out of work).

Know what you have to offer

A CEO client who was doing a CFO search said, "I was a bit taken aback when the interviewee had done a bunch of research on me and found out about my family, hobbies, educational background, and board appointments." Alan asked, "What's in it for him to work with you? Will he learn anything from you and will he be able to have your job one day?" He said, "I guess I'd better put some thought into that before doing any more interviews."

Talent Search

Be careful—many interviewers are more afraid of rejection than the interviewee, which creates lousy, ineffective interviews. You're better off offering a position that's refused by a good person than preserving ego by offering a position to a weak person who will definitely accept.

A-Players need challenges

One of Nancy's CEO clients just hired a new COO. He said, "You're not going to believe this but during our second meeting he told me that he'll be ready for my job within three years. How arrogant can he be?"

She asked him, "Why do you think he took the COO job? A-players need challenges, and your job is to help him become CEO-ready in three years if you want to keep him. Thank goodness there is enough trust and candor in your relationship that he shared his thoughts with you."

You want people with aspirations that they aren't afraid to make public.

Passion and competence lead to world-class results

Ritchie Bros. Auctioneers is the world leader in auctioneering heavy equipment. The CEO hired us to develop and deliver a leadership development program for his executive team. We weren't surprised to learn as we started working with the executive team that every single person on the team has total passion and competence for growing the business. This is the critical success factor for attracting and retaining top talent and delivering extraordinary results—which is what world-class companies do.

We have a hard time finding people more impassioned than those who work for FedEx or Southwest Air or Levi Strauss or Kiel's. We have a hard time finding people less impassioned than those who work for the Postal Service, American Airlines, The Gap, or Revlon. The former companies are doing something right to instill passion, which carries over to the customer.

There is no such thing as a company with unhappy employees and happy customers.

Bad bosses minimize application of talent

"At work, do I have the opportunity to do what I do best every day?" is one of the 12 questions in the Buckingham and Coffman research and it's strongly linked to company performance and retention.

- Often, top talent joins a company hoping to exercise talent only to find out they are blocked by their bosses.

104

- In our experience, most people are "putting in time" versus exercising their talents on the job due to bad bosses.

- If you attract top talent into your company, and they don't end up reporting directly to you, stay close to them.

Nancy was the team coach for an executive team of a high-growth division of a large financial institution. As input to the team coaching program, she interviewed each member of the president's executive team and senior management team (one level below his executive team) to get feedback on his strengths and opportunities for development.

The president was very proud of the fact that he was able to attract a top guy in the industry onto his senior management team. During the interview process the top guy said, "I joined this company because of the president. I'm stuck reporting to one of his VPs who doesn't listen and doesn't want to hear about any of my ideas to grow the business. I don't plan to stay here much longer. Neither does anyone else on the team."

Nancy suggested, "Go talk to the president. What have you got to lose?"

He talked to the president about the situation and three months later the VP retired and the top guy was reporting directly to the president.

We've mentioned "Chase Property" earlier. Keep track of top talent, give it the chance to perform, provide the opportunity to exercise talents, allow for feedback about obstacles, and then push the envelope.

Talent outs.

"SHANGHAIED" SAILORS EVENTUALLY MUTINY

If you try to impress people as old-time sea captains did sailors—force them to work—you will get neither performance nor commitment. You'll get indifferent seaman who will try to undermine you and escape whenever possible.

Attracting top talent is about building a relationship of trust consistent with the values of your company. If one of your company values is not related to helping people achieve their full potential, then you'll have great difficulty attracting top talent, because your belief system is screwed up.

Some observations and suggestions:

1. *If people aren't happy, they'll talk.*

One of Alan's CEO clients asked, "We're recruiting for a new sales and marketing VP and one of the guys on my executive team told our top candidate that this company is a terrible place to work. What should I do?" Alan said, "Spend some time with the guy on your executive team to listen to what he has to say. Then talk to everyone else on your executive team to learn more. Based on the feedback, develop an action plan to deal with all of the critical issues." Creating an environment of high performance and commitment starts at the top.

We regularly convene focus groups because they are self-sanctioning, and someone saying, "This place doesn't tell us what we need to know" is often rebuffed by six people saying, "If anything, they over-communicate. Perhaps you're just not listening."

2. *Don't delegate employee engagement to HR.*

One of our CEO clients shared his employee engagement results with his CEO forum members. He said, "I'm really depressed about these scores. We're well below our industry average. HR worked so hard and spent a lot of money last year to launch a bunch of new initiatives and our scores went down. What's worse is potential new hires are asking to see employee engagement results during the recruiting process."

We told him, "Hold your executive team members accountable for increasing employee engagement and get them to partner with HR and other external service providers to deliver results."

To reiterate, HR should *never* be the key player or linchpin in the recruitment process. They aren't equipped and the job is too important.

Talent Search

An HR VP told me once that his job was to fill vacant slots and put as many people through as many training programs as possible. "It's a numbers game," he said, winking. The only number that mattered was one less, made possible by his removal, which I began lobbying for immediately.

3. Compliance does not lead to results.

We completed a strategy execution project with the CEO and executive team of a large real estate company. During the first strategy execution workshop, the CEO kicked off the session in a loud voice. "I'm really disappointed with this team. We keep coming together and doing our execution planning but then you people never follow through on your commitments. Some of you people won't be on the team much longer if things don't change."

We wanted to know, "Does anyone have a response to the CEO's comments?" The COO said, "We're all doing the best we can to deliver on all of our commitments. We are under-resourced because we haven't been able to attract anyone onto the team. And, any time we push back on the execution plan dates you get really upset so we just keep telling you what you want to hear."

For the first time ever, the CEO realized that he had created an environment of compliance versus commitment and he apologized to the team.

So what do we find out about the recruiting game? If you buy into and adhere to the following recruitment tips, you'll create a great template for yourself and your top team.

Talent War's Talent Recruitment Tips:

• Make recruitment an essential component of every key leader's evaluation plan, including metrics for success (e.g., numbers, retention rate, promotion, and so on).

- Stay close to the talent you recruit, even if it goes to other areas and departments.

- Provide opportunity for talent to be exercised on the job, irrespective of job descriptions.[1]

- Never ever entrust recruitment to human resources, except for fundamental and rudimentary tasks.

- Provide for talent to give feedback on progress, obstacles, and the recruitment of further talent.

- Money doesn't matter so long as you are within decent market parameters. Don't throw money at what is actually a structural or intent shortcoming.

- Partner with superb recruiters *as partners*, and not as some kind of "people venders."

- "Best" and "most" lists are irrelevant. Word-of-mouth is everything. You're not trying to hire magazine writers.

- The best word-of-mouth and viral marketing for talent comes from your own people, and naturally so.

- Conformance and compliance are antithetical to the commitment that you garner from finding and nurturing top talent.

The good news is that you can begin all this tomorrow. Let's examine how leaders can build a competitive talent advantage.

---

[1]The trouble with these tips is that they are traditionally oriented toward input, such as numbers of people managed or number of clients engaged, rather than output, such as exceeding quotas. Most job descriptions are worthless in terms of allowing people to exercise talent. Fortunately, there is a quick remedy: Shred them.

CHAPTER 7

Competitive Advantage Is All Around You

Talent Builds Advantage From the Inside Out

Talent outs. We've always loved that phrase. When you boil all else away, talent gets you through the day. It is powerful, self-perpetuating, the ultimate safety net.

That's why the leadership investment in talent isn't a nicety, but a strategic requirement.

APPROACHING THE MARKETPLACE FROM A POSITION OF STRENGTH

Focus on the 10 percent of your workforce (strategic job functions—see Chapter 5) that adds the most strategic value to approach the marketplace from a position of strength.

For example, if your competitive advantage is product innovation, then your top researchers would be a strategic job function. Develop proactive strategies to ensure that your top researchers have the right skills, behaviors, and experience to execute your strategy.

One of the classic strategic errors can be seen with Kodak, the film maker caught long ago in the transition from chemically-based film to digital photography. When Kodak finally decided to truly commit to the inevitable new world, they found they had been recruiting chemists right up to that moment. Their talent acquisition was based on an outdated strategy, and seriously delayed their entry into the digital age, which required electronics experts.

All job functions are not equal. If your sales team is a strategic job function, then proactive strategies to ensure that everyone on the sales team has the right skills, behaviors, and experience to execute the strategy is critical to your success. Invest in your strategic job functions above all other job functions.

The idea of "everyone is equally important and we have to treat everyone fairly" (often put forward by HR) gets in the way of strategic thinking.

Talent Search

Strategy has to determine the talent required for the short-term and long-term future, and that talent acquisition has to reflect such strategic intent. What are you doing to ensure that dynamic is happening? It's not going to be reconciled in the human resources department.

Here are three steps to take immediately:

1. *Get to know the talent pool of your top three competitors.*

Nancy worked with the executive team of a large company in the oil and gas industry to develop a high-growth strategy and execution plan. The executive team identified product innovation as their competitive advantage. After developing the company strategy and execution plan, she worked with the executive team to develop an HR strategy to accelerate execution of the strategy.

The CEO said, "Our researchers are the most important people in our company. Without our researchers, we're out of business."

Nancy asked, "Relative to your top three competitors, what are your strengths, weaknesses, opportunities, and threats related to your research team?"

The VP research replied, "We don't know anything about the research teams of our competitors." The VP HR said, "We don't know much about the people who work for our competitors." Nancy responded, "You'll have to do a competitive analysis from a talent perspective in order to beat the competition."

2. *Get to know your talent pool by breaking down silos.*

Nancy worked with the executive team of a large financial institution to develop an HR strategy. Account managers were identified as a strategic job function, and there were 30 account managers in the current talent pool dispersed across several geographic regions.

Nancy asked, "Of the 30 account managers, how many are As (exceed expectations), Bs (meet expectations), and Cs (do not meet expectations)?" One of the VPs said, "We've never talked about our people in an open forum like this. I only know my people so I can't comment on any of the other account managers who don't report to me."

Nancy replied, "If your account managers represent your competitive advantage, you'd better get to know each and every one of them to be able to attract, retain, and develop them regardless of reporting relationships." Based on the high level review of account managers, 10 percent were identified as A-players, 70 percent as B-players, and 20 percent as C-players.

The president said, "This is unacceptable. We need an action plan to develop a 30 percent As and 70 percent Bs talent pool if we're going to beat the competition."

3. Develop a SWOT analysis for each strategic job function.

We worked with the executive team of a very successful company in the automobile industry to develop an HR strategy. Of the nine people on the executive team, three people had previously worked for their top three competitors. The sales team was identified as one of the strategic job functions to execute their high growth strategy.

We asked the executive team, "Relative to the competition, what are the strengths, weaknesses, opportunities, and threats of your sales team?" The sales VP said, "Our strength is that our sales team has more years of experience than any other sales team and we have 100 percent retention. Our weakness is they lack leadership skills because we haven't invested in their leadership development. We've brought people into sales leadership positions from the external environment and it's been a disaster. Our biggest threat is that the competition will steal away our sales team due to their frustration with their lack of career development. Our biggest opportunity is the increasing availability of world-class leadership development programs for sales people in our industry."

113

4. *Develop an action plan based on your SWOT analysis.*

The action plan for the sales team:

- Each sales person was assessed for leadership potential and interest.
- A one-year leadership coaching program was offered to all sales people with leadership potential and interest.
- They attended a week-long leadership development program for auto industry sales people.
- They participated in a six-month mentoring and job shadowing program.

THE VALUE OF A STRONG BENCH

What is a strong bench?

- If you have more than one CEO potential on the succession plan and the same for all key senior positions—give yourself options.
- If you have at least two high potentials identified for each leadership role on the succession plan.
- If you have 50 percent of your succession plan talent pool ready now to step into new roles on the succession plan.
- If you have a development plan in place for everyone on the succession plan aligned with the time frames of your strategy execution plan.
- If you have A-players in leadership roles that require A-players (e.g., high business growth areas).
- If you have B-players in leadership roles that require B-players (e.g., non-strategic areas of the business).
- If you don't have any C-players in leadership roles.
- If you realize who *does not* constitute important bench strength (expendable).

- If you understand what holes have to be filled by external recruiting and can give your recruiting partners long lead times.

What is the value of a strong bench?

1. *"Getting hit by a beer truck" is one consideration for having a strong bench.*

We've always warned clients to expect the unexpected in terms of vital talent.

Nancy worked with the executive team of a large family-owned manufacturing company to develop a three-year high-growth strategy. The CEO and his two brothers owned the business. The CEO, who was 50 years old, was the oldest brother, and he had been grooming his youngest brother, over the past two years, to become president of the company. One month after he appointed this brother as president of the company, he was diagnosed with cancer.

He said, "Nancy, I'm going to turn things over to my youngest brother immediately because I have to focus on beating cancer. My brothers are going to need your help."

Nancy told him, "You've done a great job developing both of your brothers. They will step up and run the business while you take care of your health." He died six months later knowing that his brothers would carry on the legacy of the company.

2. *More importantly, it's about accelerating strategy execution.*

Nancy was the executive coach to the CEO of a large financial institution. The CEO was 64 years old and he announced to his board that he would be retiring at the age of 65. He had a COO "ready-now CEO candidate" on his executive team who was highly regarded by everyone on that team. Shortly after announcing his retirement, the CEO was approached by another financial institution to merge. The CEO was able to delegate "running the current business" to the COO and his executive team while he focused on accelerating the merger discussions. The two companies merged and his COO was appointed CEO of the merged companies. The CEO's final year with the company was the best year of his career.

3. *It's about having leaders ready to step into new roles when required to minimize disruption to business growth.*

We worked with the executive team of a large global software company to develop a succession plan for their leadership talent pool. The company had 200 leaders in their talent pool, and when we completed the succession plan only 20 percent were ready-now to take on new roles.

The CEO said, "We won't be able to achieve our high-growth targets if we don't accelerate the development of our top talent." We worked with the executive team to develop a one-year strategy and action plan to achieve 50 percent ready-now status for their succession plan. Nine months later, one of the division presidents resigned from the executive team. Fortunately, his successor was ready-now and the CEO was able to promote his successor immediately, which minimized any disruption to their high-growth strategy.

4. *It's about having leaders ready to step into new roles when required to minimize barriers to business growth.*

Nancy was the executive coach to the CEO of a high-growth company. Due to the nature of their industry, there was very little opportunity for organic growth so their high-growth strategy was based on acquisitions. The CEO said, "I'm furious. I just came back from a board meeting and they didn't approve my next acquisition."

She asked, "Was the deal too risky from a financial perspective?"

He said, "No. They asked me if there was anyone on our succession plan ready-now to run the company if we were to do the acquisition."

Talent Search

The value of top talent is a non-balance sheet asset that should draw the attention of shareholders, bankers, and potential partners. What are you doing to maximize the return on that asset?

What gets in the way of companies having a strong bench?

1. Lack of understanding of the value of a strong bench. They content themselves with one person for one position, especially if they think they have a star.
2. Lack of knowledge of how to build a strong bench. They assume that excellent people don't need any further development.
3. Lack of passion, skills, behaviors, experience for building future leaders. There is no organizational culture or reward for the pursuit.
4. Fear of becoming irrelevant—if I have a successor then I won't be as valuable and/or I might get fired. This indicates that poor talent will never be able to pursue top talent.
5. Ego—there isn't anyone who can do my job. The ego is protective, not proud of who else can be attracted.
6. Not a priority. Too much short-term thinking, not enough understanding of the value of talent.
7. Lack of holding people accountable for having a strong bench. No monetary or other reward or consequence.
8. Lack of HR influence on CEOs to create a sense of urgency. HR doesn't have the right seat at the right table.

THE POWER OF HUMAN AND INTELLECTUAL CAPITAL

1. Intellectual capital is critical to successful strategy execution.

We worked with the executive team of a large global transportation company to develop a high-growth strategy. The company's past success was based on servicing companies in the private sector. However, the results of their industry analysis showed that the demand for their services in the private sector would significantly decline over the next three years.

The CEO said, "In order to mitigate our risks we're going to have to go after government contracts. It's low margin and it's not very exciting business but it has more certainty." The VP HR said, "We don't have anyone in our company with government contacts and experience." The CEO said, "We're going to identify the top guy in government who has the intellectual capital that we need to help us win government contracts and attract him to our company."

Six months later, they hired a top government guy and 18 months later government contracts represented 50 percent of their business.

2. Intellectual capital is even more critical in times of crisis.

Nancy was the executive coach to the CEO of a large global manufacturing company. The CEO had been in the industry for over 40 years and he had been with the company for over 25 years. His company had just lost their biggest customer, which represented 40 percent of their business. The CEO said, "I've never experienced a crisis like this before. Maybe the company needs a turnaround CEO because maybe I'm not the right guy to turn this company around."

Nancy commented, "Is there anyone else in the world who knows more about your company and your industry with a proven track record like you've had over the past 25 years with this company?" He said, "You're right. I'm the guy to turn this company around."

Talent Search

Competitive advantage is a catchphrase and bromide unless it has pragmatic meaning, and we believe it is accomplished primarily through superior talent.

3. Intellectual capital is critical to competitive advantage.

Nancy was the executive coach to the CEO of a large chemical processing company. The CEO said, "I'm really struggling with my VP of R&D. He wants more money and he wants a greater equity position in the company. I know he's the top scientist in our industry, but I just don't think he's being reasonable."

She asked, "If that guy left, do you think his team would follow him?" He said, "Yes, I think some people would follow him." Nancy asked, "Do you think you could replace him?" He said, "It would be almost impossible to replace him. And he doesn't have a successor, so that would be a problem. I guess he is being reasonable."

4. Loss of intellectual capital is a huge threat.

Nancy was the executive coach to the chairman of the board of a large retail company. The CEO, who had been with the company for 13 years, had just resigned. The chairman said, "I was very concerned about his controlling leadership style and when I approached him about my concerns he didn't handle it very well. We parted on good terms and I wish him all the best. We have a CEO successor ready-now so there won't be any disruption to our business."

Three months later, the former CEO bought the competing retail chain and became the CEO of their largest competitor.

WHY TALENT IS OFTEN SUBSUMED

Everyone is put on the planet with the ability to achieve their full potential. The degree to which they can do that, and the exact nature of that potential, has more to do with organizational leadership than most people understand or suspect.

What gets in the way of people achieving their full potential?

1. *Culture of disempowerment*

Nancy worked with the executive team of a privately held family business to develop a high-growth strategy. The CEO had recently purchased the business from his father, and he was excited about the opportunity to accelerate business growth now that his father was out of the business. As pre-work to the strategy project, Nancy interviewed each member of the executive team to identify strategic priorities and potential barriers to success. She met with the CEO to debrief the interview results, and told him, "According to your executive team, the key barrier to success is your culture of disempowerment, which starts with you. They indicated that your bullying behaviors prevent them from making decisions because they are fearful of the consequences of any mistakes they might make."

He said in a loud angry voice, "What are you talking about? That's baloney. If they don't have the courage to challenge me and make strategic decisions, then they don't belong on my team."

Nancy's reply was, "You can make it about them or you can make it about you. If you're ready to learn some new approaches to empowering your team, then I'm here for you." She worked with the CEO and his executive team over the next six months to develop their strategy and to help them shift to a culture of empowerment to speed up business results.

2. *Poor leadership*

Nancy met with one of her former clients, who was the newly appointed VP sales of a large financial institution. He said, "I can't stand my boss. He doesn't know what he's doing. I've only been in my job for six months and our results have been terrible. Sales are up but profitability is going down at a scary pace."

Nancy advised, "Go talk to your boss and give him your thoughts on what can be done to turn things around." He said, "I tried that already but he's not open to my ideas. I'm going to focus on delivering sales results and minimizing my time at the office. I know I could be adding a lot more value, but I'll just coast until my boss gets fired."

3. *Poor career management practices*

Nancy was the executive coach to the division president of a large real estate company and she asked him, "What do you want to do with your career?"

He said, "I'm ready now to take over from my boss, but I don't think that's going to happen any time soon, even though she plans to retire this year. She said I have a big ego to think that I could take over her job, and she suggested my career planning should start with getting my ego under control. Her advice to me was to keep my head down and do a good job and eventually I'll have a new opportunity come my way just like her career developed."

Nancy suggested, "Find an opportunity to meet with her boss and tell him what you want to do with your career." Three months later, his boss was offered an early retirement package and he was promoted to her job. Good thing he had the courage to talk to her boss—otherwise, he would have been stuck or left the organization.

4. *Poor performance management practices*

Nancy got a call from one of her former CIO clients. He said, "Nancy, I'm calling to let you know that I've just been fired from my job after having been with the company for three years." Nancy asked, "Did you see it coming?" He said, "I've never had a bad performance review and I had no idea." There should be no surprises if you have an effective performance management system in place.

Corporate culture often has an "immune system" that rejects foreign bodies. Leaders must ensure that new talent isn't perceived as a foreign body, but is helped to overcome the immune system.

Just as firms often make acquisitions that falter because they cannot compete with the overwhelming prevailing culture and history, so, too, do they acquire talent that faces the same entrenched favoritism. The new talent is subsumed into the prevailing iconography.

Don't be afraid to make heroic efforts to attract and integrate new talent. It creates the competitive advantage that perpetuates your strengths and obviates your weaknesses.

If you are successful in making those acquisitions and integration, the next challenge is retention. How to you keep the all-stars happy?

CHAPTER 8

The Process of Retaining Talent

Attraction is Useless Without Nurturing and Development

NONFINANCIAL INCENTIVES AND MOTIVATORS

Retention is about having a long-term view of helping people achieve their full potential. It is not directly related to financial reward, because we've found that people are most motivated by gratification from the work they produce through the application of their native talents and strengths.

Nancy was executive coach to the president of a large retail company who was on the CEO succession plan with a very successful top talent retention record, and she asked him, "What are three things that you do to retain your top talent?"

He said, "First, I have quarterly family updates and career planning sessions with each of my direct reports and with everyone on the succession plan. Second, I give people on my team a lot of recognition individually and during team sessions. Third, I foster a culture of team spirit and peer sharing so people can learn from each other and feel connected to each other."

She inquired, "How about investing in learning and growth for your people?" He said, "We don't do that very formally or proactively, so thanks for your suggestion. I'll put that on my personal action plan."

Here are six critical retention strategies.

1. *Get connected to people— in particular your direct reports and people on your succession plan. This is the single most important retention strategy.*

In the above example, the president performed quarterly family updates and career planning sessions with his direct reports and everyone on the succession plan. He established a close connection with each person because he got to know them personally. He took a long-term view of his relationship with each person on his team by discussing career planning on a quarterly basis. He also held quarterly team meetings with his top team and everyone on the succession plan to foster a team spirit. Creating an environment for people to connect with each other is also critically important. Research shows that people with a best friend at work are seven times as likely to be engaged. And employees who have a close friendship with their boss are more than 2.5 times as likely to be satisfied with their job (see Tom Rath, *Vital Friends,* Gallup Press, 2006).

2. *Give people learning and growth opportunities.*

Nancy was hired by the CEO of a large global company to coach one of his high potentials on the succession plan. The CEO said, "Nancy, we had two guys in our company who applied for our CFO position. It was a really tough decision because we felt that both guys could do the CFO job. I don't want to lose the guy who didn't get the CFO job. As part of our retention strategy, I've given him a promotion to run one of our business units and I'm going to send him on a Harvard course. I'd also like to invest in his leadership development through an executive coaching program with you."

The retention strategy worked and one year later he was listed on the CEO succession plan.

3. *Reward and recognize people for making a contribution.*

We were team coaches to the executive team of a large retail company, and we were invited to a new store opening to meet the executive team and people at all levels in the organization. Fifteen minutes before the official store opening time, the president brought everyone together in the middle of the store (about 100 people) to prepare for the opening.

The president welcomed everyone and said, "Our most important core value is we value our people. I'd like to thank all of you for your contribution to our new store opening. In particular, I'd like to reward and recognize 10 people who made an extraordinary contribution to our new store opening."

Each person shook hands with the president and accepted his or her award with total pride and joy.

4. Provide career certainty for top performers.

We worked with the executive team of a large real estate development company to develop a succession plan. Twenty people were identified as high potentials, and Alan said, "You need to tap these people on the shoulder and have a confidential conversation to let them know that they have been identified by the executive team as high potentials and share with them their career options. Creating career certainty by letting them know that they are on the succession plan is a critical retention strategy."

The CEO said, "We can't do that because word will get out and people who weren't identified as high potentials might get upset and leave the company."

We wanted to know, "Who is more important to you, your top 20 list or the people who didn't make the list?"

Talent Search

We have consistently found leadership to spend inordinate amounts of time on low-talent performers, worrying that people will feel discriminated against. What they create is an anti-retention policy, since the high-talent performers feel underappreciated and no strong loyalties.

5. Create variety for top performers.

Nancy was the executive coach to the regional VP of a large retail company. He said, "I had dinner with my boss last week and I'm really upset. He said that I might have to stay in my current role for the next two years because there isn't a successor for my role in the company. I disagree. I have a ready-now successor on my team, but my boss doesn't think he can do my job. I've been in my role for three years and I'm ready to move on. I need a new challenge, and I'm getting bored with my current role. I'd like to stay with my company, but if I have to move to a new company I will."

Nancy told him, "Develop a top-20 list of people in your company who might have some interesting career opportunities for you. Go back to your boss with the options you've created for yourself and develop an exit plan from your current role." Six months later, he made a lateral move to a head office role and his ready-now successor took over.

6. *Make people feel significant.*

Generational clashes (see Chapter 6) create retention risks because boomers feel that everyone should be loyal and stay with the company forever whether they feel significant or not. Gen X and Gen Y have a mindset of being promoted for achieving results (and therefore feeling significant), and they are more apt to leave if they don't get promoted within their preferred time frames.

Leadership must create reasonable expectations, meaning that they first have to comprehend what makes people feel significant and what their current expectations for significance are.

Nancy was the executive coach to the CEO of a large real estate development company. He said, "I'm having a problem with my new director of HR who has only been with me for six months. I did her six-month performance review last week and she asked me for a promotion because she had achieved all of her goals and objectives for the year in six months. I know I have to learn how to deal with the demands of the new generation, but I think she's being ridiculous. I told her we can talk about her request at her one-year performance review."

Nancy said, "She won't be with you for her one-year performance review if you don't address her request at this time."

INCLUSION

Diverse talent must be included in order to retain top talent. You can make an argument that employees should mirror present and future customers, or that diversity and inclusion are simply deontologically necessary.

Our point is that including diverse people improves performance and productivity by widening decision making and options. Our experience is unequivocal: Heterogeneous teams and organizations outperform homogeneous teams and organizations.

1. *Create female-friendly work environments.*

Nancy delivered a leadership development program for the all-male executive team of a large manufacturing company. The CEO said, "I know we have a problem with women in this company. We need your help in creating a more female-friendly culture as part of our leadership development program."

Nancy said that she would interview all the women on the leadership team and ask them what's working well and what's not working well in this area. He said, "We don't have any women in leadership roles in this company."

Nancy's reaction to this was, "Let's start by redesigning your recruiting and promotions processes if you want to retain women."

Be very careful about glass walls. Don't allow women to break the glass ceiling only within restricted areas, such as HR, finance, and legal. Make sure that your inclusion is also about women in top positions in manufacturing, sales, marketing, and all other key corporate areas.

Nancy also did a consulting assignment with the VP HR of a large global retail company whose primary target audience is women. The company was experiencing significant retention issues at the leadership level. Nancy asked, "What percentage of your workforce is female?"

The VP said, "Well, I'm the only female on our executive team, but our workforce is 90 percent female. I brought this issue up with my CEO, and he doesn't think it's an issue at all."

Afterwards, Nancy interviewed all of the women in leadership roles in the company and learned that the number one retention issue was lack of promotion opportunities to the executive level.

2. *Build cultural diversity at the top.*

Nancy was the executive coach to the president of a major division of a large global transportation company. She asked him, "Is one of your goals to become CEO of this company?"

He said, "That'll never happen. I'm European and the rest of the executive team are Americans. I'll have to move to a new company to get a CEO job." One year later he accepted a CEO job based in Europe, with one of their competitors.

Alan talked to a Nigerian scientist at a large pharmaceutical company. He told Alan he was going to return to Africa, though he preferred not to, because he had been told that his accent precluded a senior management position.

3. *Foster cross-cultural awareness and understanding.*

Nancy was the team coach for a global leadership team with members from Canada, United States, Mexico, Trinidad, South Africa, Chile, Hong Kong, and United Kingdom. The president said, "I have great people on my team but there is just too much conflict going on. People don't get along with each other, and I think I'm going to lose some people if I don't do something about it."

Nancy's answer to this problem was, "At the team session, we'll get each person to describe a high-performance team experience that they've had in the past. This approach will build awareness and understanding of similarities and differences between cultures. We'll then be able to develop a common vision for the team culture that people want to be part of."

The most outstanding organizations with which we've worked find it common to have someone in Chicago reporting to someone in Paris who reports to someone in Hong Kong. We're always impressed when a normal, random meeting has 12 women of a client group of 14 at a senior level. It doesn't happen often, though the odds would favor it happening at least as often as it does with males.

4. *Foster cross-generation understanding and awareness.*

We sometimes facilitate a peer forum for senior HR professionals. One of our frequent topic discussions has been "how to get boomer executives to understand the Gen Y talent pool." One of the VP HR participants shared her most successful strategy: "I asked five of our high-potential Gen Y employees to give a presentation to our executive team on what they should do to retain Gen Y. The impact of the executive team learning directly from those five high-potential Gen Ys was amazing. I was able to get the Gen Y retention strategy approved within two weeks after that presentation."

It's impossible to understand diverse people if you don't interact with them, so it's incumbent on the organization to force this interaction on a regular basis, until it is part of the norm.

THE DYNAMIC OF SKILLS, EXPERIENCE, KNOWLEDGE, AND BEHAVIOR

Development of skills, experience, knowledge and behavior is critical to retention of top talent. We separate them for these reasons and distinctions.

1. *Skills*

Nancy was the executive coach to the CFO of a large transportation company. She interviewed board members, the CFO's boss, peers, and direct reports as input to his 360 degree executive coaching program. She pointed out that the 360 degree results were very positive except for board feedback. "They describe you as arrogant, dismissive, and unprofessional during board meetings and they have some serious concerns about your inability to function at the board level. They recommend you take a director professionalism course to enhance skills at the board level."

He said, "Thank goodness, because I really don't understand their role and my role at the board meetings, so I could definitely use some skills building in that area if I'm going to survive future board meetings."

Skills are learnable competencies, which can be transferred via coaching, classroom learning, self-study, and so forth. They are adaptable irrespective of behaviors or experience, although they can be improved or discouraged by certain behaviors and experiences.

2. *Experience*

Nancy was the executive coach to a high-potential president of a large global company. His career goal was to become CEO of the company. Nancy asked him, "What's the biggest gap that is preventing you from getting to the next level up?" He replied, "Based on my 360 degree results, my biggest gap is I need head office P&L experience. I've been offered two opportunities that will become available in the next six months, and I'm really looking forward to getting the experience I need to further develop my career with this company."

Experiences are those life and business events that provide perspective and learning in real time. The accumulation of experiences creates wisdom. Experience is to skills what color is to black and white. There is no equivalent to being there and doing something. That's why the best of "in-basket exercises" and simulations can't beat the real-world experience.

Skills can enhance experiences, but experiences primarily give depth and breadth to skills acquisition.

3. *Knowledge*

Nancy was the executive coach to the newly appointed COO of a large global company. He had been the CFO of the company for five years, and his promotion to a newly created COO role was part of the CEO succession planning program.

She asked, "How do you feel about taking on the COO role given you don't have any type of operational background?"

He said, "It's so great to take on a new role in the company and to know that the CEO believes I can gain the knowledge necessary to be a successful COO. I was really getting bored of being the CFO, and I was planning to leave the company because I didn't see a career path for me."

Knowledge is the accumulation of data and information and its transformation into pragmatic, applied improvement. Combining data leads to information, analyzing information leads to knowledge, and applying knowledge in advance is an indicator of wisdom.

Knowledge augments skills acquisition and experiences, but is greatly enhanced itself from those two assets. Your knowledge of the Amazon jungle is vastly improved by experiencing it, though you also experience it better with the knowledge that you need certain medical shots well in advance and shouldn't go swimming with piranhas.

> **Talent Search**
>
> Most leaders don't appreciate all four aspects of talent development and retention. While they often overlap, careful attention to each will set you apart.

4. *Behavior*

Nancy was asked by the CEO of a large software company to work with his newly appointed COO on a 360 degree leadership development program. The CEO said, "He's been in the role for six months, and I've had a lot of complaints about him from my former direct reports. They say he's too pushy and he doesn't listen to their ideas. They are having trouble adjusting to his very driven leadership style."

Nancy wanted to know, "How does your COO feel about this feedback?"

The CEO said, "He is very impressed that I'm willing to invest in his leadership development to help him change some of his behaviors. I let my former direct reports know that I plan to invest in his development, and they are very happy to see me being proactive in getting everyone set up for success during the transition to our new COO."

Behaviors are those predispositions that manifest basic beliefs. Impatience, assertiveness, attention to detail, and persuasiveness are examples of fundamental behaviors. These can't be taught the way that skills can, or amassed in the manner of knowledge, or improved merely through exposure, as in experience.

Behaviors can be modified through coaching and feedback, and are the strongest influences on how knowledge is gained, how skills are acquired, and how well experiences are absorbed and understood. As an example: Always hire enthusiasm (a behavior). It can't be learned or experienced or amassed. It's a native predisposition.

EMOTIONAL CONNECTIONS

Emotional connection is about building trust and getting to know people at a personal level. Logic makes people think, but emotion makes them act. This is the most profound connection you can establish with people.

There are four critical areas of emotional connection that lead to high retention:

1. *CEO connection at all levels—people stay when they feel connected to the CEO.*

We acted as executive coaches and facilitators for six CEO forums consisting of more than 70 CEOs. We invited a very successful former CEO to speak to one of the CEO groups about how he rescued his company from near bankruptcy when he was promoted to CEO.

He said, "The first thing I did when I got promoted to CEO is I moved out of my big corner executive office and I set up my office in a cubicle three floors down. I wanted to get connected to our employees at all levels to build their trust and ask them to help me rescue the company. I believe that getting emotionally connected to my employees was the critical success factor. I knew about all major family events (births, deaths, graduations, anniversaries, special occasions), and I connected with people at a personal level. As a result, we had a 100 percent retention record during the company turnaround."

Talent Search

Remember, people don't leave organizations. They leave their bosses. Post this where you can see it regularly.

2. *Boss connection—people leave when the connection is broken.*

Nancy was the executive coach to the newly appointed CEO of a small manufacturing company, and she asked him, "Why did you leave your former company? It was a much larger company, and you were ready to take over from your boss, who will be retiring within 12 months."

He said, "I just couldn't connect with my boss. All he ever talked about was work. I worked with him for two years and we just couldn't agree on anything. It was his way or the highway, so I left."

3. *Peers—people stay longer when they are connected to their peers.*

Nancy was the executive coach to a woman who was partner-track consultant in a large professional services firm. She inquired, "When do you think you'll make partner?"

The consultant said, "There is no way I'll ever make partner for as long as my boss stays as my boss. He hates working with women, and he told me he doesn't think I'm partner material because I'll never fit into the old boys network."

Nancy asked her, "Why are you staying with the firm given what your boss said to you?" She said, "I love my clients and I have some great friends in my peer group to help me deal with my boss. I'll stay for as long as we keep having fun together and hopefully my boss will get transferred soon."

4. *Mentors—people stay longer if they have great mentors.*

Nancy was the executive coach to the CEO of a large global engineering company. Her question to him was, "You've been with the company for over 30 years. What kept you here for so long?" He said, "I was very fortunate to have the former CEO of this company as my mentor since I joined the company. He really believed in me and if it wasn't for him I wouldn't be the CEO today. He is one of my best friends. He's 85 years old and he still meets with me on a quarterly basis to make sure I'm set up for success. I love the guy."

Retaining talent isn't complicated, but it's not simple either. You must pay daily attention and be vigilant, no less than you are with your budget or your tactical goals.

Now we move to a fascinating aspect of the talent wars. How can you manage and control a large group of people who, by definition, are strong, rebellious at times, demand high standards, and often defy efforts to control them?

CHAPTER 9

The Aerodynamics of Leadership

Creating an Arrow and not a Flying Barn

Leadership in talent acquisition requires a combination of traits and exemplary behavior. A leader (at all levels) must serve as a navigator; as a repository of values and ethics; as a combination consensus builder and decisive advocate; and as a developer of talent who delegates and entrusts.

That sounds easy. If it were, you wouldn't be reading this.

YOU MAY BE ON THE HORSE, BUT DO YOU KNOW WHERE IT'S GOING?

People want to know:

- Where are we going in the long term (five years), medium term (two-plus years), and short term (within one year)?
- How will we get there?
- What will my role be?
- What's in it for me?

Too often, none of these questions is answered due to muddle and mire. Here is what creates the morass.

Top five mistakes leaders make:

1. *No clear vision and strategy.*

We invited a local politician (and former business owner) who was running for mayor to be a guest speaker for one of our CEO forums. One of 14 CEOs in the audience asked the speaker, "What's your vision for our city and what are your top three priorities for getting us there?" He replied, "I'm still formulating my vision," and he was barely able to articulate his top three priorities. We asked the group for feedback on his presentation and the consistent theme was, "I'm not voting for a guy who doesn't have a vision and doesn't know his top three priorities."

In the United States presidential campaign of 2008, Sarah Palin, the Republican vice-presidential candidate, received scathing criticism for being too generic in her responses and not being able to cite specific examples of her priorities.

2. *Frequently changing vision and strategy.*

We worked with the CEO and executive team of a large global software company to develop a three-year strategy. The company had been underperforming over the past two years, and there was a strong sense of urgency to develop a strategy to turn the company around. At the first two-day strategy retreat we asked the team, "What's been getting in the way of your success?"

The COO said, "Over the past two years our CEO has changed our strategy at least six times. Every time we get a bad quarterly result, we get together and change our strategy. We've lost a lot of good people because we keep changing our strategy."

Alan worked with a major hospital and found he was the fourth consultant brought in by the CEO over five years. A vice president told him, "Bill brings in a new consultant every time one of his plans doesn't work, as though the plan is fine and the rest of us just can't implement it. Funny, but the consultants don't seem to be able to either!"

3. *Not communicating vision and strategy.*

Nancy worked as the executive coach to a high-potential executive in a large financial institution. Her client requested an urgent phone coaching session on a Saturday afternoon because he had a big decision to make. He said, "Yesterday I was offered a promotion and I have to accept or decline on Monday. If I accept the opportunity I will have to move my family to a new city away from all of our relatives and it's a big decision for me."

Nancy asked him, "How does this new role fit into the company strategy?" He said, "I have no idea what our strategy is. We're going through a lot of changes right now, and I'm not even sure this new role will exist for very long. I don't think I will take it."

Alan was once told by a senior vice president at the Associated Press, "We would never share our strategy with our people! This is confidential!"

> **Talent Search**
>
> There is content and context. A pragmatic strategy must exist, and it must be communicated relevantly to everyone in the organization.[1]

4. *Not involving people in vision and strategy development.*

We worked with the CEO and executive team of a large manufacturing company to develop a one-year execution plan for their three-year company strategy. At the first executive team meeting, the VP Sales and Marketing said to the CEO, "You developed our strategy with a consultant and you presented it to us at our last quarterly meeting. We don't really understand your strategy, so I'm not sure how I'm going to get my sales team excited about developing a one-year execution plan. They know our customers and industry better than you do. We'd better get their input on the strategy if we want them to make it happen."

The frontline people are always the best sources of input for critical elements affecting the operation's success with customers, suppliers, and other stakeholders. Don't impose a *fait accompli*. Use these people in the creation of strategy.

5. *Not aligning strategy with structure.*

Nancy worked with the CEO and executive team of an industry leading, large global company on strategy execution and aligning the company organizational structure to accelerate strategy execution. The CEO reviewed with her the existing organization chart and the new very complex organization chart that he had developed.

---

[1] See *The Power of Strategic Commitment*, by Alan Weiss, Josh Liebner, and Gershon Mader (Amacom: 2009). This book offers lengthy descriptions on the dual needs of content and context for strategy.

Nancy asked, "Why do you have so many dotted and solid lines going from each box? Your strategy hasn't changed drastically from previous years so why so many changes?"

He said, "Are you telling me that I'm headed for a train wreck with this new organization chart?"

She replied, "Strategy drives structure and role clarity. Let's work with your executive team to simplify your organization structure to attract, retain, and develop top talent and accelerate business results."

Winston Churchill said, "We build our houses and then they build us." He was talking about Parliament, but his message is highly relevant. We can't afford to allow structure to dictate function.

STRATEGY AS A DAILY GUIDE AND FILTER

What is the converse of the mistakes above? Here are five tough decisions leaders need to make to ensure successful talent flow.

1. *Letting go of some talent.*

We worked with the CEO and executive team of a large manufacturing company on strategy development. The CEO said, "We're going to focus on our top three customers over the next three years and abandon our other customers. We can't afford to keep losing money on our other customers. If this strategy fails, we'll learn from it and we'll move on to develop a new strategy."

The VP HR asked, "Are we going to let some of our talent go when we implement this strategy?"

The CEO said, "We'll do whatever it takes. They'll come back to us when we need them in the future."

Leaders need to set priorities, because they can't ensure work for everyone. Just as some clients need to be fired or sent elsewhere, so does some talent in order to preserve top talent.

142

2. *Letting go of a B-player when you need an A-player.*

Nancy worked with the newly appointed president and executive team of a division of a major transportation company. The president said, "I've met with each person on my executive team and I've learned that our VP sales is a great guy. He has been with the company for over 20 years and he delivers results, but he's just not going to take us to the next level."

Nancy remarked, "If you're accountable for taking your division to the next level, you're going to have to find an A-player for the VP sales role."

We've found sterling performance reviews for key people based on their attitude and, in one memorable case, arriving early in the morning to get the coffee started.

> **Talent Search**
>
> Choosing talent is not an on/off switch, but rather a rheostat. Maintain contact, which will sometimes be brighter, sometimes dimmer. But in the end, you want to obtain the shining light.

3. *Waiting for top talent when he/she is available.*

Nancy was the executive coach to the CEO of a large global retail company and she told him, "You know you have to replace your COO and you've identified the perfect person for the COO role (and your potential successor). He's taking a year off between jobs to spend time with his family and he'll be available within six months. Wait for him and you won't have any regrets."

Six months later, the CEO hired the new COO and a year later the COO was appointed CEO. If you have the right person for your strategy, it will serve you to wait for him or her.

(It's also a good idea to grant sabbaticals to retain top talent that might otherwise burn out. These are sometimes paid time off, sometimes "loaned" provisions to non-profits and community organizations, and so forth. Not every horse can run at full speed in every race and retain a sense of challenge and superb conditioning.)

4. *Facing gaps on your team.*

We worked with the CEO and executive team of a large transportation company to develop a three-year high-growth strategy. The executive team agreed that 30 percent of their high-growth strategy would be achieved through acquisition, and we asked them, "Have you had success in the past through acquisition?"

The CFO said, "No, we've invested a lot of time and effort and we've had lots of failures. I think we need someone on the executive team who has that experience, because I don't." Three months later, the CEO brought in a new CFO with acquisition experience and the existing CFO was transitioned out of the company.

Organizations with effective succession planning and career development initiatives will know early and accurately what gaps have to be filled, allowing for methodical acquisition of key talent and not panicked reactions in precarious times.

5. *Getting people on your team to accept new top talent.*

Nancy worked as the executive coach to the CEO of a large high-growth retail company. His goal was to create a new COO role so that he could transition to chairman within a year and promote the COO to the CEO role.

He said, "I've been working with my VP Sales as my right-hand guy for over 20 years, and he probably thinks I'll be promoting him to the new COO role. He's a great VP sales, but he's not CEO potential. He's not a strategic thinker, he's not good with numbers, and he hates coming to executive team meetings."

Nancy instructed, "Make it about you and not about him. Tell him that you plan to bring someone into the company who is even smarter and better than you are at running high-growth companies and strategy execution. Focus on your gaps—not his gaps—and you'll get his buy-in to bringing in top talent."

Every organization has an immune system, which tends to reject outside talent. The good news is that you know that, so provide the proper preparation, acclimatization, and acculturation to avoid this fatal problem.

ACCEPTING DISSENT BUT NOT REBELLION

Involvement in strategy development and execution planning is critical to getting commitment from people and retaining top talent. Leaders need to create an environment of trust and candor to encourage people to share their points of view and feel empowered to influence.

However, once strategic decisions are made, everyone must commit to the strategy in order to ensure success. Compliance isn't good enough. We love both New Yorkers and Australians because there can be vast disagreement, which is never taken personally, and final commitment to a decision wherein everyone's voice was heard, no matter how shrill or countercultural.[2]

Here's how to ensure dissent but not rebellion.

1. *Always clarify who owns the decision, or "Who has the D?" (Rogers and Blenko, "Who Has the D?"* Harvard Business Review, *January 2006) to get everyone on the same page and avoid rebellion.*

One of our clients who is the CEO of a publicly held company described "Who has the D?" for his strategy to his executive team: "I had a meeting with our board chair to get final approval on our company strategy. He wanted me to show him all of the changes I made based on board input. I showed

---

[2]Women are much worse at this than men because they tend to take opposition and rejection personally, whereas men see it as "just business." Sorry, that's our experience and observation, as a man and a woman writing this book.

him every single change that was made and then he approved the final strategy."

The CEO wanted to make sure that his executive team understood that the board had influence and final decision-making approval on the strategy. Once the strategy was approved, the role of the executive team would be to execute and not further debate the strategy.

We worked on a strategy project with the board and management team of a large private manufacturing company. The former CEO was on the board, and we asked the newly appointed CEO, "Who has the D on the strategy?" He said, "I don't know, but we'd better find out because I know I'm not on the same page as the former CEO regarding the future strategy of this company."

At the strategy session, the chairman of the board clarified that the CEO and management team would have the "final D" on the strategy because they had to execute. At one point during the session the former CEO said, "I'd like to veto that decision because I strongly disagree with that strategy."

The chairman said, "No veto. Let's move on." Clarify "Who has the D?" to avoid major conflicts and rebellion.

Talent Search

There are two types of group meetings. One involves open discussion with the decision maker listening, perhaps participating, and making the final decision. The other involves the same dynamic, but with the group consensus determining the decision. The problem is that too many people think they're in the second scenario when they are actually in the first.

2. *Explain how decisions are made to avoid rebellion.*

We do a lot of team effectiveness workshops with executive teams, and I always introduce decision-making tools using the following scenario. It's a lot easier to avoid rebellion if people understand how difficult it is for leaders to make tough decisions.

Scenario: CEO introduces strategic initiative called "eat the vegemite"

Our CEO has just come back from a board meeting and he's been asked by the board to increase productivity by 30 percent. He learns that several of his CEO colleagues have discovered research evidence that suggests that getting all employees to eat vegemite every day will increase productivity by 30 percent. Vegemite is a healthy yeast extract that most people in New Zealand eat every day (and the author ate every day when she lived in New Zealand for three years while she obtained her PhD).

The CEO has the following five decision-making approaches to choose from in order to make his decision on how to increase productivity by 30 percent:

D1: I decide.—The CEO decides on "eat the vegemite" with no input from others.

D2: I decide with individual input on new ideas.—The CEO gets individual input on new ideas to increase productivity by 30 percent from people on his team before making a decision.

D3: I decide with individual input on "eat the vegemite."—The CEO gets individual input on "eat the vegemite" from people on his team before making a decision.

D4: I decide using a team compromise approach.—The CEO holds a team meeting to get everyone's point of view. He makes a decision even if some people disagree with the "eat the vegemite" initiative.

D5: I decide using a team consensus approach.—The CEO holds a team meeting (or several meetings if necessary) to get everyone to understand why and reach agreement on the "eat the vegemite" initiative.[3]

---

[3]This is based on Victor Vroom's famous work at Yale on the decision-making styles available to leaders. See Vroom and Yetton, *Leadership and Decision Making*, (University of Pittsburgh Press, 1976).

Choosing which D1-D5 approach would be most effective is based on (1) amount of information available; (2) amount of time available; (3) impact on people; (4) need for learning and growth.

Rebellion occurs most often when people don't understand how and why decisions are made and when they aren't involved in decision making to the extent they feel they should have been involved. Also, they need to know the rules.

3. *Don't accept rebellion. Hold people accountable.*

We worked with the CEO and executive team of a large global company to develop a three-year strategy and execution plan. At our first strategy session, one of the business unit presidents said, "I think we have to change how we do things. We come together as a global team two times a year and we commit to our strategy and execution plan. But we then go off to our own regions and we don't follow through on our commitments."

We wanted to know, "What gets in the way of people following through on commitments?"

He said, "We all want autonomy, and we each do what we think is right for our regions and there are no consequences. We're going to meet quarterly from now on, and we're going to monitor our strategy and execution plan. You won't be on the team if you don't stick to the plan."

Sniping is much easier when one has no vested stake in the outcomes. Create vested stakeholders who need success. Remember, a team wins or loses together. A committee has members who can win or lose individually. Isn't it a pity you hear so much about "the strategy committee" rather than "the strategy team"?

MICRO- AND MACRO-MANAGING

Leaders with control manias and mico-managing styles lose top talent faster than water in a sieve. Don't forget, people don't leave companies, they leave bosses. A micro-manager is a repulsion force.

Here are some examples of control mania behaviors.

1. *Telling people to stop thinking.*

Nancy was the executive coach to the CEO of a large financial services company.

He said, "I've had some retention problems on my executive team, and I think it's because I'm a control freak. I'm getting a lot better. I used to tell my team to stop thinking and just listen to me to get it right."

Alan once worked with a CEO who finished everyone's sentences for them, no matter what their specialty. No matter that he was usually right, after a while his people stopped preparing in depth. Alan told him to shut up and take a count of two before speaking after someone else had stopped speaking. Suddenly, his staff was back on point.

2. *Telling people what to do and how to do it.*

Nancy worked with the CEO and VP Marketing of a large global company to develop a global marketing strategy. The VP Marketing and Nancy met with the CEO to kick off the project. Nancy asked, "What are the objectives of the project and how will we measure success?"

He said, "Don't give me any of that consulting speak. I'm going to tell you what to do and how to do it because I know my company and I know what's going to work." Nancy inquired, "What do you need us for if you have all of the answers already?" He said, "I guess you're right. Let's go back to objectives and measures of success."[4]

3. *Not giving up decision making.*

Nancy was the executive coach to the president of one of the major divisions of a large retail company. He said, "I think

---

[4]Objectives, measures, and value comprise conceptual agreement, vital to project success and pioneered by Alan Weiss. See his book, *Million Dollar Consulting,* fourth edition, McGraw-Hill, 2009.

I have to quit. I've been with the company for three years and I can't stand working with my CEO anymore. He doesn't let me make any strategic decisions, and my team knows that I'm a lame duck because I have to go to the CEO for all major decisions."

She asked, "Have you tried talking to him about the situation?"

He said, "No, one of my colleagues got fired for challenging the CEO about his decision-making style at one of our executive team meetings." A year later, the president resigned from the company and started up his own company.

> **Talent Search**
>
> A leader who micro-manages creates a legion of micro-managers below. The entire benefit of winning the talent wars is that you should never have to micro-manage!

4. *Focusing on details instead of the big picture.*

Nancy was the executive coach to a newly appointed regional VP of a large financial services company. She interviewed the VP's direct reports as input to her 360 degree coaching program. A common theme that emerged is reflected in the following comment from one of her branch managers: "She's a micro-manager, and she's driving us crazy. She should be focused on the big picture and developing a strategy for growing our business, not making sure we sweep the floors and tidy the boardroom for her visits."

Macro-managing is about evaluating progress toward strategic goals, not about reading Kaizen charts on the plant floor or daily calls made by the sales force. Take a look at your time allocation over a week (keep a journal, like the attorneys do, of 15-minute increments). How much of your time is spent on macro issues, and how much on micro?

We bet you'd be surprised at the results, since almost all of our clients have been.

5. *Focusing on perfection, not progress.*

Nancy was the executive coach to the CEO of a large global company. His key development opportunity was to strive for progress not perfection. The culture of the company was high burnout and turnover because of his control-freak style.

During the first coaching session he said, "I'm really proud of my team. We had a major proposal that had a Monday morning deadline and we pulled several all-nighters over the past week and weekend to deliver a perfect proposal. I know we'll beat the competition."

Nancy asked him, "Do you really think you need to pull all-nighters to beat the competition?"

He said, "That's the way I've always done it, so I expect my team to follow me."

There is often a boot camp mentality of blind allegiance to pain and corporate suffering. The idea is that no "t" should go uncrossed, no "i" undotted. We've never seen a proposal or contract fail because of the lack of a dot, sorry.

Leaders need to shift to a coaching approach to leading in order to overcome control mania behaviors and build future leaders.

Once we delivered a two-day "Advanced Coaching Skills" leadership development program for the CEO and executive team of a large global company. The board and CEO recognized that the executive team needed to shift from a command and control-freak leadership style to a more empowering approach in order to retain top talent and accelerate business results. At the end of the two days one of the division presidents said, "My job is going to be a lot easier now that I can push decisions down and ask questions instead of telling people what to do. It's not going to be easy to make the transition, but I know it's the right thing to do to grow my people."

And, besides, it's much less stressful to be a macro-manager and coach than a micro-managing mania nut.

Seven coaching steps to prevent you from being a control freak:

Scenario: CEO in a coaching conversation with his CFO

Note—CEO statements are underlined. CFO statements are in quotations.

1. Listen first. <u>What can I help you with?</u> "I'm having some challenges with my controller."

2. Listen 80 percent of the rest of the time. <u>Tell me more</u>. "He's been with us for six months, and I think I'm going to have to let him go. He's just not delivering results."

3. Ask questions. Don't tell him what to do. <u>What are your options?</u> "I think I have three options: (1) keep him for another 90 days to see if things improve; (2) fire him; (3) find a new role for him in the company."

4. Let the other person evaluate the options. <u>What are the pros and cons of each option?</u> "If I keep him for another 90 days, I'll feel better about giving him another shot at turning things around, but it'll take up a lot of my time to coach and mentor him. If I fire him, I'll be able to promote one of his team members into the controller role, but it'll send shock waves throughout the team because the controller has only been here for 6 months. If I find a new role for him, he might be able to deliver in another area of the company, but there is a risk that I'll move the problem to a new area in the company."

5. Ask for a decision. <u>What will you do?</u> "I plan to keep him for another 90 days and if it doesn't work out I'll look at the other options."

6. Share your views but don't override the decision even if you disagree. <u>I think you're just delaying the inevitable. Six months is ample time to assess a controller.</u>

<u>However, I fully support your decision to keep him for another 90 days</u>. "Thanks for your support."

7. Follow up and hold him accountable for dealing with the issue. <u>Are you making progress with your controller?</u> "No, he's gotten worse over the past month, so I plan to terminate him next week. You were right about six months being ample time to assess the controller. I'll move faster next time."

The aerodynamics of leadership is about taking the 50,000-foot view and managing from above, looking for progress toward the destination—the strategic goals. Now let's apply that macro approach toward developing the all-stars.

CHAPTER 10

Counterintuitive Development

Focusing on Top Talent, not Remedial Help

Developing talent is about continuously developing the skills, behaviors, and experience of individuals and teams to build competitive advantage. This never ends and, in fact, becomes more complex and demanding as conditions continue to evolve.

MINIMIZING DYSFUNCTIONAL HUMAN RESOURCE INVESTMENTS

Here are some strategies we've found efficacious to focus on the top, not the bottom, of the talent ladder. Note that there are three major components to job excellence, as indicated in Figure 10.1.

Strategy A. Focus on developing top talent versus remedial help.

Nancy was the executive coach to the newly appointed COO of a large global company. She asked, "What happened to your predecessor?"

He said, "He wasn't delivering results so the CEO did everything he could to rescue the guy. Apparently, he sent him

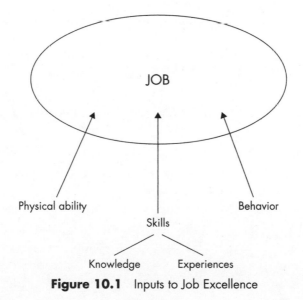

Figure 10.1 Inputs to Job Excellence

on a Harvard course, he assigned him an executive coach, and the CEO mentored him weekly, but he just got worse so they let him go after 14 months in the job. The CEO said I've only got 90 days to demonstrate that I can deliver results so that's why you're here."

Obviously, the CEO learned that investing in getting people set up for success versus remedial help for people not delivering results is a much better approach to development.

Talent Search

Sending people to programs doesn't guarantee growth. You have to choose the right people, at the right time, for the right development. This isn't about getting a ticket stamped, but about individualized excellence.

Strategy B. Set priorities to maximize your return on investment on development dollars.

We worked with the executive team of a large global company to set priorities for talent development to accelerate strategy execution over a three-year period.

Here is a summary of the top-five development priorities for the three-year period:

1. The executive team—individual 360 degree coaching program and two-day executive team leadership development program based on coaching program results (year 1).
2. The people on the succession plan—individual 360 degree coaching program and an internal mentor is assigned (year 1).
3. All people in leadership roles—all leaders attend a four-day in-house leadership development program (year 2).
4. Ten percent of the workforce that adds the most strategic value (i.e., strategic job functions)—accelerated career plans and development plans are executed (year 2).

5. A-players at all levels—accelerated career plans and development plans are executed and an internal mentor is assigned (year 3).

As you can see, the approach was both longitudinal and comprehensive—broad and deep.

Strategy C. Make leaders versus HR the decision-makers.

Nancy was the executive coach for the executive team of a large global company. One of the high-potential executives on the succession plan asked, "I'd like to work with you as my coach. How do I make that happen?"

Nancy said, "Talk to your boss, and if he says yes, let HR know and we'll get started." Three weeks later she got a call from him and he said, "The good news is my boss said yes. The bad news is the VP HR said no because he felt that coaching wasn't the right approach for me and he's the final decision-maker."

Nancy asked, "What will you do now?" He said, "I just handed in my resignation. If my career development depends on the VP HR who knows nothing about my job, then I'm not going anywhere in this company."

We insist that any kind of "management dashboard"[1] must include clear responsibility for developing talent as a priority. This can *never* be delegated to HR or any staff function.

RECOGNIZING THE ALL-STARS

Recognition is key to developing all-stars, in particular in the following key areas. We don't mean identifying, since we've covered that earlier. We mean rewarding, highlighting, and supporting those who are your best and brightest.

---

[1] A common term for the range of indicators that a manager should be responsible for improving.

1. *Providing new challenges.*

Nancy was the executive coach to the VP Marketing of a large retail company and she asked him, "What is the key thing your company has done to recognize you as an all-star over the past seven years?" He said, "I've been given and I've asked for a new challenge every two years. I'll stay here for as long as I continue to get new challenges every couple of years."

Never let function follow form. That is, don't constrain your best people by the box you've created on the organization chart. Instead, give them plenty of latitude to gain results in a variety of ways.

> **Talent Search**
>
> Job descriptions should never be about tasks, which are arbitrary inputs, but rather about outcomes and results, which allows high performers to initiate new ways to achieve dramatic results. No good people belong, or are comfortable in, a box.

2. *Funding development opportunities.*

Nancy was the executive coach to the COO of a large global company. She asked him, "In addition to coaching, what is your development plan for this year?" He said, "My CEO is sending me to the Harvard Advanced Management Program. I'll be acting CEO while he's away for four weeks during the summer. And, I'll be doing a trip to Asia with my CEO to job shadow him for three weeks. I know I'm the only one at my level who is getting these development opportunities and I feel very fortunate."

Just because you can do something faster or better yourself (at least, in your perception) is insufficient reason not to delegate to people who need the experience in order to develop the skills and to practice the behavior.

3. *Offering flexible work arrangements.*

Nancy was the executive coach to the CEO of a large manufacturing company. The CEO said, "I've got a real problem
with my VP Sales. He has asked me for a four-day work week.
His job requires him to travel a lot and his new wife wants to
spend more time with him."

Nancy responded, "If he's an all-star and you want to keep
him, you'd better give him what he's asking for." The CEO
approved the four-day work week request and a year later he
said, "It was the best thing I could have ever done. The VP
Sales is still delivering amazing results, and he's a lot happier."

Don't view objections and suggestions as irritations of
ambitious people. View them as intense signs of interest from
the future of the company.

4. *Offering sabbaticals.*

Nancy was the executive coach to the VP HR at a large
retail company. He was on the succession plan, and he had
been with the company for 10 years.

He said, "I really feel like I need a sabbatical. I think if I take
a three-month break from this place I'll get re-energized, and
when I come back I'll be able to take on new challenges with
a lot more energy and enthusiasm. Otherwise, I'll have to make a
move because I really need a break from this company."

Nancy asked, "Has anyone ever taken a sabbatical in your
company?"

He said, "No, but I did plant the seed with my CEO last
year and he couldn't handle it at all."

She advised, "Be straight with your CEO about your situation and make your request again. Present him with a business
case for offering sabbaticals for high potentials in the company
as a retention strategy." He got his sabbatical approved and
since then other all-stars have been able to take sabbaticals.

Organizations such as IBM have provided sabbaticals or
full-paid leave to work on community efforts or for nonprofits
for years, with stellar results.

CREATING ACCOUNTABILITIES FOR DEVELOPMENT

We've found that there are six main areas of accountabilities for development.

1. *Board: The board chair is accountable for board and CEO development.*

- Board Development

Nancy was the executive coach to the CEO of a large global publicly held company. The CEO said, "My board has a bunch of dinosaurs on it and they don't understand their role. Our board meetings are horrible because the management team doesn't think the board adds any value and the board doesn't respect the management team."

Nancy told him, "Ask your board chair and a couple of other influential board members to take the Director Professionalism course (offered by the National Association of Corporate Directors) with you. You'll learn a lot together and you'll be able to improve board effectiveness." The board chair got back from the course and asked each board member and management team member to take the course as soon as possible.

Alan worked for over a year with the large board of the American Institute of Architects to help them with their priorities and governance responsibilities. These were professional architects, so why would they automatically know how best to serve on a board?

- CEO Development:

According to the October 2008 Harvard Business Review article "Evaluating the CEO," by Stephen Kaufman, the CEO should be evaluated on five main areas: leadership, strategy, people management, operating metrics, and external relationships. The board is accountable for ensuring that development plans are in place to ensure CEO success in all five areas.

Nancy was the executive coach to the chairman of the board of a large privately held company. The board chair said, "Our new CEO needs some coaching help. He's causing quite a bit of upset with the management team because of his very direct style. I'm going to tell him that he has to work with you to get fixed up before he causes more damage."

Nancy said, "Talk to him about how valuable coaching has been for you and offer me as a resource to help him. You can hold people accountable for behavior changes, but you can't push development on people. He has to be ready to accept help." The CEO agreed to meet with me, and we decided to do some leadership development coaching work together.

CEOs are among the least developed of all leaders because it's assumed they've reached a stage where they have no more to learn! Alan once worked with the CEO of a major health care organization, who was superb at his job. When the three-month coaching effort was concluded (mostly validating how good he was, but covering a few places to improve still more), he sheepishly asked, "Do you think I could make it at Merck?" (which was one of Alan's major clients and very highly regarded for its professional management). I assured him, he could have.

2. *CEO: The CEO is accountable for executive team development and for holding executive team members accountable for the development of people.*

Nancy was introduced to the CEO of a large global publicly held company who wanted to improve the leadership effectiveness of his executive team. He said, "Nancy, I want you to work with all of the guys on my team to get them to become more empowering leaders."

Nancy asked, "How about you?" He said, "My board chair is a great mentor so I don't need any coaching."

Nancy replied, "You are the exemplar for your team. If you're the first person to go through the 360 degree coaching program, then your team will follow you based on the improvements they see you making." The CEO agreed, and two months later he shared his 360 degree results and 90-day action plan with his team. Everyone was impressed with his commitment to improving his leadership abilities, based on their feedback, and they all signed up for the 360 degree coaching program.

After completing the 360 degree coaching program for all executive team members, Nancy worked with the executive team to develop a succession plan aligned with the three-year company strategy. The CEO said, "We're going to monitor our succession plan on a quarterly basis just like we do our strategy execution plan. And I'm going to check in with our high potentials on the succession plan every quarter to ensure that they are developing according to our plan. I'm also going to propose that we make 25 percent of our performance rating based on our employee engagement scores."

Talent Search

The most powerful influence for leadership development and voluntary investment of time and energy is the top person demonstrating that he or she has the need, so it would be unusual for someone else not to have the need.

3. *Executive team members: They are accountable for ensuring all development takes place (including their own development), as per our "Strategy B" example.*

Nancy was the executive coach to the CFO of a large global company. He said, "I'm having a real problem with getting my controller to follow through on his development plan. He says he's too busy and he just can't afford to take the time away from work to go to the leadership development program. I don't want to put too much pressure on him because he's already so stressed out."

Nancy advised, "Give him a specific deadline for attending the program and help him put a plan in place to ensure he'll be able to attend. Share your positive experiences with the program and why you feel he'll benefit from the program." The controller signed up for the program and met his development plan deadline.

Normally, more effective development takes place when a team engages in it together, rather than individuals attending separate programs. The latter sets up a competition and ticket-stamped mentality. If you don't think all of your people are ready or suitable for joint team development, *then it's time to either change your people or change your perceptions.*

4. *Leaders at all levels: Work with all direct reports to ensure development plans are executed.*

Nancy was the executive coach to the VP marketing of a large global company. She said, "Nancy, I'm on the succession plan. Every year for the past two years my boss approves my attendance at a leadership development program and then two to three weeks before I'm due to leave he makes me cancel my participation because we're too busy. This year I want to make sure I get to go."

Nancy advised, "This year request a meeting with your boss and your CEO to confirm your participation in the program."

She said, "My boss will never agree to that meeting."

Nancy said, "Give him two other options. You'll request a meeting with the CEO on your own or you'll resign." She got approval to go to the leadership development program, and she attended that year.

5. *HR: Accountable for partnering with the CEO and executive team to ensure that the talent development strategy is executed. This often takes place in the form of quarterly presentations to the board and executive team.*

HR is also accountable for providing tools, advice, and guidance in alignment with the overall company talent development plan.

Nancy was the executive coach to a regional VP of a large retail company. She said, "My boss is the COO and he's going to retire next year. He hasn't said this to me, but I think I'm next in line for his job. I talked to our VP HR, and she thinks I should be listed on the succession plan for her role. She doesn't think the COO role would be a good fit for me. I know they have a succession plan, and I don't know why they won't tell me about my future opportunities."

Again, Nancy advised, "Request a meeting with your president and ask him to share the information with you. Let him know what you've learned so far." As a result of her meeting with the president, he became her mentor. Six months later, she was promoted to COO and her boss was given an early retirement package. A new person was appointed to the VP HR role.

(As we've mentioned at earlier junctures, HR isn't always up to the task. Either, build an HR department that can handle this important work or find other ways to do it.)

6. *Individuals: Develop and follow through on a development plan to achieve your career goals.*

Nancy was the executive coach to the COO of a large retail company. The CEO had announced his retirement a year earlier than expected, and the COO had been identified as the only internal candidate for the CEO role. The board made plans to complete the external search and make a decision on the new CEO within six months.

Nancy said, "Let's agree that your job over the next six months is to get the CEO job."

She said, "I only have six months left and there is no way I can get any more development dollars from the company."

Nancy asked, "In addition to your current development plans, what do you need to do to get the CEO job?"

She said, "I need to learn more about influencing boards, and I need to get connected to other experienced CEOs. I'll pay with my own personal money for taking a board course and joining a CEO forum right away."

Organizations must foster a culture of self-responsibility for development. This is where HR, the immediate superior, and external consultants can help show options for people who are either too busy or too modest to investigate and choose developmental and experiential opportunities.

SHARING SUCCESS AND CREDIT

Sharing success and credit is important for all-stars to acknowledge their significance to the company and to accelerate their development.

Here are five strategies for sharing success and credit that you can implement immediately.

1. *CEO connection.*

Nancy was the executive coach to the CEO of a large global company. He said, "I feel like I need to spend more time with high potentials in my company, but I'm not quite sure how to do it without causing upset to people who are not identified as high potentials at this time."

She asked him, "Would you rather retain top talent or minimize upset?" We developed a plan for him to have quarterly dinners with high potentials listed on the succession plan and an annual two-day retreat with high potentials to work through significant business issues.

It's not uncommon for us to recommend weekly breakfasts, special receptions, and attendance on high-profile trips and client visits to create better connections with the CEO.

2. *Cross–functional, high-potential team projects.*

Nancy was the executive coach to the newly appointed CIO of a large retail company. He said, "Our employee engagement scores went down by 10 percent this past year, and I need to do something about improving our scores."

Nancy advised, "Work with your leadership team to identify six to eight all-stars in your IT organization. Pick the person with the strongest leadership skills to lead the team and report to you directly for the purpose of this project. Empower the team to develop and execute a plan to raise the scores by a minimum of 10 percent this coming year."

The all-star team achieved a 20 percent increase in employee engagement for the IT department, and they were all given an additional one-week vacation for their efforts that year. All-stars love challenges, and they need to be empowered and rewarded for delivering results.

This has the added benefit of destroying silos and private turf to foster better collaboration at all levels.

Talent Search

Outstanding people love competition. The idea is to create healthy competition so that *all* can win, instead of one person winning *at the expense of someone else,* which is the default setting in too many organizations.

3. *Daily recognition and praise throughout the year.*

Nancy was the executive coach to the CEO of a large financial institution. He said, "Our employee engagement results indicate that we need to get better at recognition and praise in this company. I have to admit that I'm not very good at giving out recognition and praise. I've never been given a lot of recognition and praise so I haven't had a lot of role models in my career."

Nancy told him, "Make it a daily habit over the next 30 days to give out frequent and tailored recognition and praise to three people each day. This could take the form of sending an e-mail message, leaving a voicemail message, sending a card, or giving a verbal message to people. Notice the impact you have on people and let me know how it goes."

She met with the CEO a week later and he said, "It's the most amazing thing I've done in my entire career. The joy I see in people's faces when I give them a simple pat on the back is so rewarding to me."

The legendary "management by walking around" is highly suspect. The key is this: *What are you doing and saying while you're walking around?*

4. *Recognition awards and bonuses.*

Common approaches include trips, cash, and extra time off.

Nancy once asked one of her CEO clients (the sole owner of a very successful private company), "What do you do to recognize and reward your all-stars?" He said, "Every year I pay for the top 50 performers in my company to go to Hawaii for a week with their spouse. This is an additional one-week vacation, and I give them a healthy vacation cash limit."

Be careful that you don't simply reward the behavior you would have otherwise received and expected. Ensure that you're providing rewards for "stretch" behavior, and for which everyone can qualify (win/win, not win/lose).

5. *Peer Ranking.*

Nancy was a university professor for seven years in the business faculty at Simon Fraser University. Each semester, the 50 professors in the business faculty were ranked based on teaching ratings. Each year, the top 10, including Nancy, were sent a letter congratulating them for achieving top 10 status. They were invited to special lunches with the dean of the faculty. Nancy got to know the top 10 ranked professors quite well, and she learned a lot from them about how to continuously improve her teaching; she also shared her experiences with the others.

GE and other organizations have made it a point to always establish a "bell curve" review of their talent. The key is that even the people on the lower portion of the bell curve are better than those at higher levels in other companies!

CHAPTER 11

Six Strategies to Win the War for Talent

Winning Mere Battles is Insufficient

We want to leave you with specific actions that you can adopt, implement, and embrace immediately to win the war for talent. You may win some and lose some, but you must prepare for all of them. In the longer term, it's the war that needs to be won even if interim battles may be lost.

CREATE A LEADERSHIP STYLE THAT IS CONSISTENT AND TRANSPARENT

Building Trust Around You

In our experience—and this is supported by many in-company surveys—employees value consistency of leadership above all. That is, "toughness" or "autocratic" or other seemingly pejorative attributes can be tolerated if a leader is consistent and uniform in behavior and reactions. But employees throw up their hands and throw out their accountabilities when leaders are inconsistent and entirely situational.

What are some of the qualities of consistency and trust?

- Reward and punishment are doled out based on continuing criteria. The sales force doesn't get a bye for unethical behavior because "you have to forgive them, they're sales people."
- A priority is a priority is a priority. They don't fluctuate, and you can understand what the criteria are (e.g., seriousness, or urgency, or growth, or some combination thereof).
- If the customer is important, then you act that way. You take the customer's call, put emphasis on customer service, reward people for customer innovation, and so forth.
- Crises bring out the best in consistent behavior instead of creating inconsistent behavior. While Johnston & Johnston and then-CEO Jim Burke have received legendary status for their handling of the Tylenol tampering crisis, not many people realize that those values of honesty, accountability, and rapid communication were

in place and observed for years with zealous embrace. (We've worked with both J&J and Andersen, and what happened later with the tampering crisis and with Enron came as no surprise. Values are not situational.)

- Projects and initiatives proceed from a start through a building process to a finish. Things don't peter out, or wind up in dead-ends, or arise out of spontaneous combustion. People can track events. The talk in the hall *is not* "Here we go again!"

Consistency creates reliability and dependability. That is, followers will grant you trust and confidence. I know how you will likely react to events, what you will probably initiate, what criteria and values are important to you.

Therefore, I can *trust* you if you keep commitments, clarify expectations, and face tough issues with consistency.

> **Talent Search**
> You can't destroy the grapevine. But you can put in place more powerful, transparent communications mechanisms.

What are some of the qualities of transparency and candor?

- Decision making is open and clear. Everyone understands the criteria and how risk and reward are assessed. Most importantly, people understand who will make the decision, and they feel that they have influence over decisions that will impact their ability to do the work.
- Politics are minimized. People receive or are denied based on the merit of the argument and the objective evaluation, not based on department, longevity, or who had your ear last. We've encountered far too many executives, particularly in human resources, who proclaim, "I really manage the CEO. I control his time and determine her priorities." That is the definition of opaque.

- Promotions, appointments, and selection are viewed as merited by virtually everyone, with the possible exception of a few disappointed candidates. No one is accused of bribing, conniving, or sleeping their way into their position.
- The CEO walks the talk *and* talks the walk. That is, while the top person's actions are entirely consistent with values and beliefs, he or she also talks about those actions and beliefs with pride and candor. Instances of support and violation are equally, honestly discussed.
- The focus is on cause, not blame. The CEO influences rapid and objective problem solving, not public humiliation or finger pointing. After all, the event occurred on *everyone's* watch.

Transparency is an accelerant, because people do not have to invest time trying to figure out why and where something happened, or what the justification and causes may be. They can tell by looking.

Therefore, they can *believe* you if you talk straight, demonstrate accountability, and show respect.

In a major insurance company, we encountered the top vice president for sales condoning his sales people's desperate habit of forging names on applications in order to meet quota deadlines even when prospects were not physically available to sign binders. The CEO agreed that we needed a public demonstration of his position, not merely a backroom scolding.

At the next executive meeting of the top 40 officers, we brought up several questionable practices for discussion and saved this for last. After a heated debate, almost entirely against the vice president's position, the CEO made it abundantly clear that the practice was unethical and would no longer be tolerated. It became the vice president's accountability to prove the practice had been abolished by the next meeting.

Remember that procedures and actions that you do not openly oppose you passively support. If we had not raised the forgery issue publicly, the assumption would have been that the CEO favored it, or it had been stopped on the hush-hush because the CEO was worried about outside pressure.

What you don't take a position on, others will assign a position for you.

CREATE ACCOUNTABILITIES FOR TALENT CREATION AND RETENTION DOWN THE LINE TO ATTRACT, RETAIN, AND DEVELOP TALENT

The greatest impact on employees is their immediate supervisor or manager and the commensurate environment that is created. In Alan Weiss's doctoral dissertation in organization psychology, he used Merck, Hewlett-Packard, and Marine Midland Bank (now a part of HBSC) to determine whether innovation on the job was a function of behavioral predisposition or environment.

In other words, if behavioral predisposition of various types (e.g., highly assertive or highly persuasive individuals) resulted in greater creativity and innovation on the job—and assuming these were desirable traits for the subject companies—identifying these people in the search, recruitment, and interview phases of talent requisition would be vital. However, if environment trumped behavior, then environment would be critical.

The results were unequivocal, and are supported by our consulting work over the past two decades: The direct manager and the environment he or she creates has by far the strongest impact on encouraging or discouraging desirable behaviors.

Consequently, we've also concluded that to win the talent wars, the CEO must engage in a strategy of holding all key people accountable for the attraction, acquisition, retention, development, and nurturing of top talent. While the CEO can't do this alone, the CEO alone is the key avatar of such behavior.

Nancy worked as an executive coach with the CEO of a major global distribution company, who had nine direct reports. The CEO's biggest concern was not having enough leadership talent to grow the business. And he had given up hiring externally due to several hiring failures over the past five years. He was also under pressure from his board to hire externally to create a more global mindset within the company.

"Do you hold your direct reports accountable during performance reviews for attracting, retaining, and developing world-class talent?" asked Nancy.

"No, we focus on business results in this company and that's how we've been successful in the past," said the CEO.

"Past doesn't equal future in the war for talent," she replied. "You need to move away from the old sink-or-swim leadership development approach to one of coaching and mentoring to retain your people." CEOs must make sure that competencies are developed in growing internal talent as well as integrating external hires if the war for talent is to be won.

Nancy worked for more than six months with the CEO and the direct reports on 360 degree executive coaching. Each person developed a 90-day action plan to accelerate leadership development. The CEO shared his own 90-day plan with the board and his team. Each direct report shared his plan. The CEO was then able to hold direct reports accountable for their own development and the development of their people.

The greatest causes of stress on the job—which, in turn, are the greatest human resource expenses in terms of disability and absenteeism—are these:

1. The feeling that one has no idea what will happen in the future at work.
2. The feeling that one has no influence over that future no matter how one's talents are applied or exercised.

Unfortunately, in many organizations, those talents are never even sought or applied by management. Instead, arbitrary job descriptions take precedence with their monotonous litany of tasks to be performed and activities to be completed.

To attract and develop top talent, people have to be free to exercise all of their skills in terms of the results they can generate. The more one exercises the multiplicity of abilities that exist, the more gratification results from the work.

Here is our definition of empowerment: *The ability of the employee to make decisions that influence the nature and direction of the work.*

Are your subordinate managers, let alone your direct reports, empowering your best people to strive for results and to make those decisions *that influence the nature and direction of the work?* Ask yourself these questions:

1. Are we measuring results (output) or tasks (input)? Do we measure sales calls or closed sales, financial reports or financial initiatives?

2. What do we value? Do we reward positive behaviors and not just victories, or must one win to be appreciated? (At Calgon, Alan introduced an award for "the best idea that didn't work," personally presented during an annual conference by CEO Fred Kerst. The idea was to reward behavior in a good cause, even if the outcome wasn't a win. It was immensely popular.)

3. Do my direct reports have emphasis areas that include talent acquisition and development? (And what about *their* direct reports?) Unless there is a formalized assessment and metric for talent improvement, then it becomes a nicety that doesn't matter in terms of recognition, promotion, and so on. You must hold subordinates' feet to the fire of talent creation.

4. Are we adding responsibilities as fast as people can handle them, or do we restrict them to the organizational restriction box? As long ago as the late 1960s, Prudential Insurance was instituting programs for hotshot recruits who could move in a faster track in home office management. Their promotions, titles, perks, and pay were not restricted by the normal human resource

bureaucracy. If you weren't being frequently transferred in the International Paper Company, you simply weren't on a fast track. At GE, if you didn't go overseas to manage a unit, you weren't considered top drawer. Chase had a famous, locked "Chase Property" room, which allegedly had very few keys (one in the possession of David Rockefeller) with the photos of the all-stars who were to receive accelerated assignments and rapid challenges. The CEO at Tastemaker, a leading food flavoring company owned by Monsanto at one time, made sure that even his vice president of human resources had line P&L responsibility by also serving as the managing director for the Mexican operation.

> Are you allowing your corporate cogs and wheels to grind through people irrespective of talent contribution, or are you fast-tracking the best and the brightest? That's never a responsibility for human resources (which seldom houses the best and the brightest) but for you, the CEO, exclusively.

5. What message am I personally sending about nurturing talent? With whom have I surrounded myself? Are they the longstanding family retainers, or are they diverse people, including newer, high energy, rapid achievers? When you look around the room do you see only a reflection of yourself?

Working at the American Council of Life Insurance many years ago, Alan worked with a dozen breakout groups split up among 250 CEOs and COOs of major American insurance companies. The 20+ executives in each room had a common group of concerns at the time: Why aren't we appealing to a wider demographic? Why is term insurance so popular, even though it's a poor alternative, especially for younger people? Why aren't we trusted more by those looking for investment options?

"Look around," suggested Alan. "You all look alike. Why would someone who doesn't look like you trust you?"

That applies to customers, clients, employees, and especially to current and prospective talent. If you want to win the talent wars, the talent has to believe that they have a place in the operation.

MARRY CAREER DEVELOPMENT AND SUCCESSION PLANNING

We've seen far too many organizations that seem to treat succession planning and career development as if they were oil and water, or pastrami and mayonnaise.

Succession planning is top-down, and career development is bottom-up. They are supposed to meet, just as a bridge started on opposing shores is supposed to align into one usable roadway. The engineers don't say, "Hey, a couple of inches or a foot off is good enough for government work." Their tolerance is in fractions of inches or centimeters. But that's because there are the same engineers on both sides of the river.

Usually, succession planning is driven by the executive team seeking to create "bench strength," and career development is driven by human resources people seeking to justify their training budget. These are inherently antipodal goals.

For the record:

Career Development: A methodical approach to providing the skills, knowledge, and experience that individuals require to qualify for higher positions commensurate with their talents and objectives; to perform optimally at their current jobs; and to achieve a sense of fulfillment and gratification from receiving an investment in their learning and growth. When conducted correctly, career development is seen as an employee *benefit*. When conducted poorly, career development is seen as senseless time in classrooms being exposed to irrelevant material.

Succession Planning: A methodical approach to determining which positions will be needed in the future and what the sources will be to fill those positions with talent, either from inside the company or outside the company, and to identify what resources are best kept at their current positions and which others may be subject to transfer or deliberate attritions. When conducted correctly, succession planning provides for timely and excellent replacements for planned or unplanned openings. When conducted poorly, succession planning is a political turf battle that results in the wrong people in the wrong positions.

> **Talent Search**
>
> When succession planning and career development are not "married" or synchronized, you have the proverbial "bridge to nowhere" in your own organization.

The CEO is the sole person who can ensure that these two very important undertakings result in an aligned roadway, because otherwise there are not the same engineers on both sides of the river. These programs have to mesh just as highly calibrated gears create maximum power with minimum friction (see Figure 11.1). Succession management and career development also need to be aligned with the execution of the company strategy. For example, quarterly strategy reviews should include a review of the outcomes of the succession management and career development plans.

Career development should maximize current performance while supporting the potential for future performance. Succession planning should be able to call upon the results of career development to create *choices* for future selection. If a company is left with just a single candidate for a key job, then something is amiss. (Even the need for an external candidate should have been anticipated in the process.)

When Jack Welch was CEO of GE, he created a legendary approach to such bench strength. Larry Bossidy, just one of

Figure 11.1 Meshing Gears of Succession Planning and Career Development

many examples, as a very senior GE executive left to become CEO of Allied Signal—and had a distinguished career there—without GE missing a beat. When George Wendt had to be replaced as the head of the most profitable division of GE, the credit operation, it was done smoothly. When Welch himself retired, Jeff Imelt was chosen from a field of several high-potential successors. Some who did not get the top job left to take other top jobs, and were themselves smoothly replaced by the GE succession system without skipping a beat.

In Figure 11.2 you can see that talent acquisition originates in three areas: those ready now, those requiring additional career development, and those who have to be obtained from outside the organization.

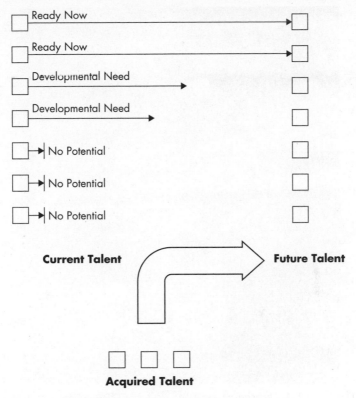

Figure 11.2 Succession Planning Process

External candidates are positive, so long as they are not the rule (meaning you are not developing people internally and/ or that you are not providing incentive for advancement from within), but need to be planned. Gerstner was parachuted into the CEO role at IBM with a great result, but John Scully moved from Pepsi to Apple as CEO with horrible result. External candidates need to be acquired *well in advance* of the intended opening that they will fill. For a company of IBM's size, the failure to have an internal candidate is an indictment of the succession planning system and the board and the executive team. The same could be said of Hewlett-Packard, Merck, and others. (Merck reverted to a long-time insider after an outsider failed.)

Only the CEO can make sure the bridge is constructed with quality, aligned, and then usable. You can't win the war for talent by asking people to jump in the river at the last minute.

BECOME THE LEADING ADVOCATE AND AVATAR FOR TOP TALENT ACQUISITION

Every truly great athletic coach takes personal responsibility for finding, recruiting, and finalizing the acquisition of top talent. Top college football coaches spend most of their time off-season romancing the best high school talent, *and* their families, *and* their supporters.

When Bill Belichick of the New England Patriots decided he needed a veteran, retired linebacker named Junior Seau, who was 3,000 miles away surfing, Belichick contacted him personally. Seau noted in a televised interview, "It wasn't a scout, or anyone in the administration, or an assistant coach, or even the general manager. It was the man himself."

When we are asked to donate major sums to specific charities, we respond with the most money and the quickest response when the executive director or chair of the board contacts us. If you desire a major gift from a major donor, you need a major player. We don't respond well to people reading scripts, or uncertain of themselves, or unable to make certain decisions and commitments, or not passionate about their cause.

Talent Search

A zealous desire to attract, retain, and nurture talent becomes infectious and contagious. You don't want any immune system thwarting that.

You are not circumventing or undermining your recruiters or subordinates or human resource department. *You are assisting them in their mission.*

Every year, you should be personally responsible for the acquisition of a few key people, the number depending upon the size of your organization and the succession chart discussed above. You can't hold others responsible for jobs you choose not to do, nor can you truly evaluate the obstacles others claim to encounter and the resources they claim to require unless you are in the midst of the effort yourself.

Hyatt Hotel executives became famous for taking the roles of bell staff, room services people, front desk clerks, reservationists, and so forth for a few days every year. The guests had no idea about the substitutions. This tactic was a key for the most senior people to appreciate and plan for the actual guest interactions, challenges, requests, unreasonable behavior, and total experience.

You can't learn that in a report or during a meeting. You can't find out about the scarcity of minority candidates, or the competition for female graduates, or the perquisites provided for top scholars, or the tangential but relevant interests of the candidates unless you are talking to them, visiting them, and listening to them.

Here are our suggestions for the CEO role as exemplar and avatar of top talent acquisition.

- Publicly accept the accountability for recruiting talent each year.
- Assign accountabilities to your direct reports and evaluate them on their success no less than their meeting financial or ethical standards.
- Serve as a mentor to a few of the top people brought on board.
- Evaluate the success of ongoing recruiting *and retention* every quarter with the top team.
- Ensure that the organization is a magnet for talent by:
  - A positive and supportive working environment
  - A diverse work force with a variety of different role models
  - Competitive compensation and benefit plans

- Obvious and high-impact community involvement
- Supportive family and dependent policies
- A strong image in the press and community groups
- Strong testimonials from recent talent acquisitions
- Strong relations with key academic talent sources
- Showcase new talent with choice assignments and visibility.
- Talk about talent acquisition in speeches and memoranda.

The finest leaders have historically led from the front. They get on the horse, a visible target, and say, "Follow me!" The don't try to rally the troops by urging them forward with the guarantee that "I'm right behind you!"

One final but vital consideration: The boldest and best, the extraordinary CEOs, make the acquisition of talent a strategic and board consideration. It wasn't unusual to observe the board at Merck or Monsanto discuss the role of talent in the achievement of strategic goals, the sources of the talent, and the accountability for its acquisition.

The CEO can either grumble and moan about still anther chore imposed by a distant board, or can lead the charge with the understanding that the board is right on target and this is the most critical issue facing the company.

As in anything else, with talent acquisition, lead, follow, or get out of the way. Only one of those makes you an extraordinary CEO.

VIEW TALENT HOLISTICALLY, EMBRACING LIFE BALANCE

Alan often serves as a visiting lecturer and adjunct professor, and he found himself on one such occasion at Boston College addressing an extension program class on life balance. The 40 participants were all highly successful people, between 35 and 55 years of age, and at various stages of happiness or unhappiness about their lives.

At one point, an attorney stood up and said, "I work 18 hours a day on the law, in my office, at home, and at the request of clients on weekends or off-hours. I love the law. I love helping people through the law, and I'm passionate about it. Why do I need 'balance' beyond my work?"

"Do you have a wife and children?" asked Alan.

"Yes, I'm married ten years and have two kids, six and seven."

"And are they as happy as you in their lives with what little time is left for them, or do they tend to complain that they don't have enough of your time?"

Total silence ensued.

We relate this story because acquiring and *retaining* talent requires a holistic approach. Law firms are finding that the torturous 80-hour weeks are no longer being endured by top recruits, despite the allure of making partner early. Hedge funds have found that key managers reasonably determine that making $40 million for a 60-hour week is better than making $60 million for an 80-hour week. And even that traditional bastion of unreasonable and slave-like labor, the hospital intern system, is under attack for insane work demands that actually decrease the quality of patient care and result in poor decisions and diagnoses.

Some talent is young and fresh from college, some is veteran and established in other work forces; some is unattached, some is family-oriented; some is singular in intensity in entering a new position, some is heavily involved in personal activities and social events; some is local, some is from distant climes.

Different people have different needs. Just as a blanket motivational program will never work (despite what the human resource people will claim as they purchase off-the-shelf programs), one-flavor approaches to delighting new talent won't work.

The literature is very clear: People are most motivated by gratification from the work and the exercise of their innate talents. Hence, leadership should provide environments, management, and support systems that provide for the application of those talents on the job *and the freedom to apply other talents off the job*. The ancient leadership bromide that employees have only two key dimensions, sleeping and working (and good luck fitting in anything else), is long dead.

More and more companies are providing lunchtime learning activities, from the building of personal negotiation skills to the appreciation of Native American art forms, and from music appreciation to etiquette and grooming. The more the organization becomes a source for holistic growth and learning, the more it is an accomplice and not an obstacle for one's life fulfillment. Microsoft pays for employees with spouses to go to Dr. John Gottman's workshop on "The Art and Science of Love," for example.

Companies such as Levi Strauss and Hewlett-Packard are famous for providing the opportunity for community volunteerism, charity work, and environmental improvement. Thus the organization is a *channel for and enabler of* individual life balance needs.

As an extraordinary CEO, you can provide the leadership and incentive for such life balance and holistic need. What are your family values? What is *your* obvious involvement in the community? What is your clear connection to the arts? What do you visibly do to support worthy causes? To what degree do the media report your chairing an activity, or donating time (money is too easy), or coaching a team, or leading an initiative?

No one in your organization believes what they read or what they hear. They only believe what they *see*. And the most visible person is *you*.

Top talent is far too complex and valuable to shove into an arbitrary box, common track, or generic program. Nor can the approach be solely one of work responsibility and growth. You must engage them in the fulfillment of their life goals.

Others will copy your example. What example are you providing?

ACCEPT NOTHING LESS THAN EXTRAORDINARY LEADERSHIP AND TALENT

Finally and most critically, you cannot accept anything but outstanding talent in key positions throughout the company. That sounds like common sense at best or a platitude at worst, right?

However, we've spent a good portion of our consulting lives telling CEOs that they must fire someone. Usually, it's been someone who is undermining the team, surrounding himself or herself with inferiors, underperforming, and uncollaborative. But CEOs tend to adopt a savior mentality: Not on my watch.

One of the greatest myths is that the CEO should be responsible for everyone succeeding. This is simply false. The CEO is responsible for tough people decisions and is the one person who can make them fearlessly and quickly.

> **Talent Search**
>
> The leadership must be willing to make tough decisions, because no one else is in a position to do so. The talent advantage is decided by making high quality, tough decisions. Diamonds emerge from great pressure.

Alan worked with the CEO of a major health organization, who had four direct reports. The top lieutenant in charge of marketing and sales was a tyrant, dressing-down people in the halls with streams of obscenity, openly denigrating his peers, and promulgating an attitude of "us against them" within his own company. A succession of coaches had been hired and summarily fired. This was clearly a borderline personality disorder and he was killing the firm.

The CEO at first refused, as he had with all the former coaches. "Just work with him," he'd plead, offering more money, "I have an obligation to help him to realize his talent and remove the obstacles to his success."

"You are killing the company, not him," Alan pointed out.

189

"How can that be?!" shouted the CEO, "everyone knows I'm supportive, approachable, flexible...."

"Because," Alan cut him off, "everyone makes the only logical conclusion they can, that you approve of his behavior because you do nothing about it, and your passive acceptance of it indicates that he is simply doing your dirty work while you remain above the fray. People think you're behind this, and it's only a matter of time before the board thinks you two are working in concert on the good cop/bad cop approach."

One week later, the lieutenant was offered a handsome severance package in return for his resignation.

Nancy worked with the CEO of a major retail company, who had six direct reports. The chief operating officer was not delivering results despite biweekly coaching meetings he had with the CEO over the past two years. At weekly executive team meetings, the COO would complain about other departments and would always have excuses for his team's inability to deliver results.

"What are you going to do about the COO?" is what the CEO heard from other members of the executive team. He didn't know how to respond. The CEO explained to Nancy, "If I fire him, he'll fall apart. He won't be able to get on with his life. I know he has financial difficulties. I don't think I've done enough to help him."

Nancy pointed out that the CEO was the exemplar for all his direct reports. "World-class companies have world-class people," she explained. Courage is about making these tough decisions. Others will be inspired by the action, and the COO would have to get on with his own life.

Three weeks later, the COO returned from an extended business trip and was offered a severance package in return for his resignation. The CEO called Nancy to thank her for giving him the courage to act on something he should have done two years prior. Three months later the COO became CEO of a smaller company, which was a wonderful fit for his talents.

We've spent inordinate amounts of time convincing CEOs to fire people. Why is that?

It's because CEOs are accepting less than extraordinary leadership and talent. The flip side of locating, attracting, recruiting, and nurturing top talent is that you must expect to performance. Sometimes, despite the best efforts, this fails to transpire.

Don't throw good money (or time, prestige, and energy) after bad.

We've found that these are the major reasons why CEOs accept less than top performance:

- Long-term retainers who spark a sense of mutual loyalty.
- Belief that the person will never recover from the feedback.
- Lack of emotional fortitude/courage.
- The right language and time to "do it and say it."
- Failure to establish metrics for *superb performance.*
- No downside or penalty for poor performance.
- Unclear goals.
- Inattention.
- Failure to shift expectations as conditions change.
- Insularity and a willingness to believe what's said, not actually done.

There is a delicate balance between dictatorial rule and setting high standards. It's never fair to ask people to do the impossible, but it's always fair to ask them to raise the bar to new heights. Our response to the complaint "But we've never been able to do that" is "What's your point?"

We'll conclude with a set of behavioral guidelines for the CEO who truly believes the job entails obtaining and building extraordinary talent. We've formatted this so it's easy to pull out of the book or copy and place on your desk.

The CEO's Role in Winning the Talent Wars

1. Determine what positions demand extraordinary leadership and talent *now and in the future.*
2. Assign responsibility and monitor progress in career development matching succession planning needs.
3. Take a personal role in attracting outside talent to fill the areas that internal succession cannot fill.
4. Personally interact with prized recruits on a frequent basis. Make them company property.
5. Diligently weed out nonperforming people in all key capacities.
6. Establish very tough standards for new talent, and cut your losses where, inevitably, some will not measure up. (No one bats 1,000 in recruiting.) If you have success one-third of the time you are above average, according to Jack Welch, former GE CEO, in his book *Winning.*
7. Recognize and reward outstanding contributions publicly.
8. When necessary, make heroic efforts to attract top talent that wouldn't ordinarily be available to you.
9. When people are performing in an outstanding manner, *continue to increase expectations of performance.* The worst position is to allow good people to coast.
10. Invest most heavily in the continuing development of top talent and extraordinary leadership, not in remedial work, because that is where the greatest ROI resides for your organization.

Fortunately, winning the war for talent is not a zero-sum game, where only one person can win. And it has nothing to do with terrain, technology, or tenor of the times.

It has everything to do with you.

Index

INDEX

Index

Index

INDEX

Index

Index